When can resorting to war be justified, and when not? Who is a legitimate target of attack, who is not—and why? Answering these questions, Uwe Steinhoff gives a succinct, precise and highly critical account of the present status of just war theory and of the most important and controversial current debates surrounding it.

Uwe Steinhoff is Senior Research Associate in Philosophy, The Leverhulme Programme on the Changing Character of War, University of Oxford.

D1557355

ON THE ETHICS OF WAR AND TERRORISM

The Changing Character of War Programme is an inter-disciplinary research group located at the University of Oxford, and funded by the Leverhulme Trust

On the Ethics of War and Terrorism

UWE STEINHOFF

OXFORD
UNIVERSITY PRESS

OXFORD
UNIVERSITY PRESS

Great Clarendon Street, Oxford OX2 6DP

Oxford University Press is a department of the University of Oxford.
It furthers the University's objective of excellence in research, scholarship,
and education by publishing worldwide in

Oxford New York

Auckland Cape Town Dar es Salaam Hong Kong Karachi
Kuala Lumpur Madrid Melbourne Mexico City Nairobi
New Delhi Shanghai Taipei Toronto

With offices in

Argentina Austria Brazil Chile Czech Republic France Greece
Guatemala Hungary Italy Japan Poland Portugal Singapore
South Korea Switzerland Thailand Turkey Ukraine Vietnam

Oxford is a registered trade mark of Oxford University Press
in the UK and in certain other countries

Published in the United States
by Oxford University Press Inc., New York

British Library Cataloguing in Publication Data
Data available

Library of Congress Cataloging in Publication Data
Data available

Typeset by SPI Publisher Services, Pondicherry, India
Printed in Great Britain
on acid-free paper by
Biddles Ltd., King's Lynn

ISBN 978–0–19–921737–3

Contents

Acknowledgements   vii

Introduction   1
1. Legitimate Authority   7
2. Just Cause (Including Subcriteria) and Right Intention   23
3. Innocents, Double Effect and Proportionality   33
4. Non-combatant Immunity and the Definition of
   Non-innocence and Innocence   61
5. The Ethics of Terrorism   109

Notes   139
References   153
Index   159

Acknowledgements

Chapter 5 draws on material originally published in the following article: Uwe Steinhoff, "How Can Terrorism Be Justified?", in Igor Primoratz (ed.), *Terrorism: The Philosophical Issues*, 2004, Palgrave Macmillan, pp. 139–56, reproduced with the permission of Palgrave Macmillan.

I thank Volker Gerhardt, Georg Meggle and Igor Primoratz for valuable support and stimulating discussions, and the participants of the two conferences *The Ethics of Terrorism & Counter-Terrorism* (ZiF, Bielefeld, 2002) and *Civilian Immunity in War* (CAPPE, Melbourne, 2003), which were organized by the latter two philosophers, for criticism and suggestions. I owe special thanks to Jeff McMahan for written comments on an early draft of the manuscript, and in particular to Colin King for correcting my English translation of the original German book and for his saintly patience with respect to my pedantic questions on minor linguistic nuances. I would also like to thank OUP's Dominic Byatt for his encouragement. The appearance of this book, which is a revised version of the German original, has been made possible by the *Oxford Leverhulme Programme on the Changing Character of War*. My final thanks go therefore to the *Leverhulme Trust* and to my colleagues in the *CCW* programme.

Buenos Aires, July 2006

Introduction

The very idea of an ethics of war is suspect to some people—either because they believe that "all's fair" in war or, on the other hand, because they think that there simply cannot be such a thing as an ethically condonable war or an ethically condonable kind of warfare. That there should even be an ethics of terrorism, and hence some legitimate kind of terrorism, is likely to appear not merely to some as a position which is in equal parts absurd and immoral. According to common sense, terrorism is the paradigm of senseless, or, at the very least, of downright illegitimate and detestable violence.

But common sense is not necessarily a reliable standard in these matters. In the course of history it has often enough adjudged obviousness to opinions which were by no means obvious, but rather completely unfounded and, moreover, wrong. Consequently, when it comes to ethical questions of some importance—and war and terrorism probably are phenomena of some importance—one is well advised to advance philosophical analysis against common points of view and to question pre-existing, socially established frameworks of discussion and prejudices, instead of docilely accepting them. At least, one is well advised to do this if one is concerned with exercising one's own responsibility. For we are not only responsible for our deeds; we are also, and foremost, responsible for the formation of our beliefs—since everything further follows from this. It is true that, lately, some circles have sworn to an abstention from reflection, on the grounds of a kind of unconditional solidarity—similar to an abstention of reflection on the basis of religious belief which was once declared to be no less decent. But such ideas are perverted and ignorant, and they belong to an age before the Enlightenment. Intellectual integrity is the condition of every other form of integrity.

Thus it is a lack of intellectual integrity, in the form of breathtaking double standards and hypocrisy in the assessment of war and terrorism (and in the assessment of different perpetrators), which constitutes the main target of this book. For the purposes of illustration I shall cite certain present-day examples, in particular those pertaining to the Middle East conflict. Yet these references to current affairs do not, to be sure, alter the fact that this is first and foremost a philosophical enquiry—an enquiry in which the ethics of war and of terrorism are to be clarified in a *fundamental* way. In the course of this enquiry I shall treat traditional just war theory, which goes back to the Catholic Church fathers Thomas Aquinas and Augustine and has been further developed by other thinkers. This theory will be discussed, yet by no means adopted; rather, some of its central points are rejected here.

Just war theory distinguishes the legitimacy of entering or continuing, respectively, a certain war (*jus ad bellum*) from the legitimacy of a certain kind of warfare, that is, the legitimacy of the manner in which war is waged (*jus in bello*). In short, the *that* of war is distinguished from the *how* of war. This separation, however, is only analytical, since the justification for entering into war is also dependent upon the way in which the war will most likely be conducted.

Six criteria are usually given for the *justification of entering a war* (or for continuing a war):

1. A *legitimate authority* (king, president, parliament and the like) decides on the entrance into war.
2. One has a *just cause* for entering into war (e.g. defence against an aggressor).
3. One pursues the war with the *right intention*, namely for the purposes of a just cause (thus, for instance, one does not harbour the plan of not ceasing conflict once the aggressor has been thwarted or possibly even punished, and of getting further advantages for oneself, such as the increase of one's own power or the acquisition of territories or resources).

4. The war fulfils the condition of *proportionality,* that is, it is a proportionate means, which is to say that it does not create more mischief than it averts.

5. The war also fulfils the condition of having *prospects of success* (in the sense of prospects of victory).

6. The war is the *last resort* (*ultima ratio*), that is, there are no other promising alternatives available.

For *the legitimacy of the conduct of war,* in turn, there are above all *two conditions* which must be fulfilled, namely:

1. The condition of *proportionality* must be fulfilled (one is not to bomb a country "into the Stone Age" if victory may also be had less destructively).

2. The principle of *non-combatant immunity* must be observed, that is, some distinction must be made between combatants and non-combatants or, respectively, between legitimate and illegitimate human targets of a direct attack.

In the first two chapters we shall deal with the criteria of *jus ad bellum.* In the *first chapter* I shall argue, contrary to the tradition of just war theory, that every single individual is a legitimate authority and has the right to declare war on others or the state, provided only that the individual proceed responsibly in his or her decision processes, that is, that one proceed in circumspect and rational consideration of relevant information and moral aspects. This is merely a thoroughgoing application of a perspective which is enlightened, liberal and oriented to individual rights, a perspective which I am at pains to adopt throughout. In contrast, the view that such rights are attributable only to the state and its representatives, but not to the individual, is pre-Enlightenment and pre-modern, namely medieval, or modern in the bad sense of belonging to a metaphysics of the state and having certain totalitarian tendencies. One might, of course, be inclined to object, independently of the moral question, that for purely analytical reasons there can be no such thing as an individual war. The expression "war", one might say, is to be reserved for states, or, in any case, for communities. But if not only states but even small Indian tribes can wage war, there is no reason why the number of the participants in the war could not be reduced even further. For example, in the Western *Jeremiah Johnson* (Warner Brothers, 1972),

Robert Redford plays a trapper whose Indian wife is murdered by another Indian tribe. He thereupon vows revenge and attacks the men of this tribe again and again, in order to kill as many of them as possible. The Indians, in turn, dispatch single warriors (their code of honour prohibits them from attacking a lone enemy in a group) to kill him. I do not see why one should not say in this case that the single trapper is engaged in a war with the entire tribe. Nevertheless, whoever is reluctant to use the expression "war" in this context can replace it with "armed conflict". For the purposes of my argument, the distinction is moot.

In the *second chapter* we shall turn to the other criteria of *jus ad bellum*. It will become apparent that the criterion of just cause contains all other criteria, with the exception of the criterion of right intention, as subordinate points. The question as to the legitimacy of the cause, then, cannot be clarified independently of these other criteria. Besides, the criterion of right intention is interpreted here in a significantly more tolerant way than is the case in the tradition of just war theory.

The following three chapters are concerned with *jus in bello*. The *third chapter* is dedicated to the question as to how strictly the principle of non-combatant immunity is to be interpreted. The so-called contingent pacifists like to make this principle absolute and conclude, with reference to the fact that at least in modern war innocents are also always killed, that all modern wars are reprehensible. (There are "strong" or "radical" pacifists who claim that war is wrong *in and of itself*. I will deal only with the arguments of contingent pacifists, calling them for convenience simply "pacifists".) Just war theorists, on the other hand, appeal in this question to the doctrine of double effect with which they maintain the view that only the direct and intentional killing of innocents is absolutely prohibited, but not the mere acceptance of their death as the side effect of an attack on a military target. I shall demonstrate the untenability of this doctrine while at the same time rejecting the pacifist argument; in this part of the argument I shall have recourse to proportionality considerations, among others.

In the *fourth chapter* I shall discuss different approaches to the definition of "non-innocence" and "innocence" in the context of war and determine their respective scopes and relevance, as well as the relations between them. It will be shown that non-innocence and innocence in war, and the consequences resulting from non-innocence or innocence for the legitimacy or illegitimacy of an attack on non-innocents or innocents, is a very complex and multilayered phenomenon indeed, one which cannot be reduced to a single principle. From this follows, among other things, a critical assessment of certain clauses of the laws of war, in particular of those clauses in which aggressors and defenders are conceived as having, in principle, equal rights.

In the *fifth chapter* I turn to those phenomena commonly described as terrorism. Certain definitions of "terrorism" which invoke a double standard or are simply philosophically inadequate are rejected (a first step in this direction, however, is already undertaken in the first chapter). The result of the explication efforts undertaken in this chapter may be formulated in the following definition:

Terrorism is the strategy of intimidating or impressing others than the immediate victims or targets of violence by the repeated threat, made credible by corresponding acts, of the repeated killing or severe harming of innocents or the repeated destruction or severe harming of their property. *Terrorist acts* are such severe attacks on innocents or their property which constitute part of such a strategy.

(Pending the defence of this definition in the fifth chapter, however, we may understand "terrorism" in a rough sense as the direct attack on innocents for political purposes.) Different approaches to the justification of terrorism are analysed and it is ultimately shown that terrorism is condonable in certain, albeit extreme, circumstances. Such circumstances emerge for strong parties under greater difficulty than for weak ones; in fact, for strong parties they probably do not obtain at all. Therefore, for states, and for strong states in particular, there are in nearly all circumstances only three legitimate and recommendable means for fighting subnational terrorism: abandonment of double moral standards; focused persecution of crimes (insofar as the committing of a punishable crime—and not of an act of justifiable resistance—may be demonstrated); and the inclusion of those who have previously been excluded from justice and liberty.

1

Legitimate Authority

Among all just war theorists, probably no one has emphasized the criterion of legitimate authority as much as A. J. Coates has recently done. He explains:

The criterion of legitimate authority has become the most neglected of all the criteria that have been traditionally employed in the moral assessment of war. Nowhere is this more evident than in the popular assessment of contemporary terrorism. For many the central moral issue raised by terrorism is that of non-combatant immunity.... To regard terrorism in this way, however, is to make an enormous, and almost always unwarranted, moral concession, since the distinction between combatants and non-combatants (or "guilty" and "innocent") is one that applies only to a state of war.[1]

And wars, one must presumably conclude, can only be waged by legitimate authorities (a view which, as far as I can see, has found no second exponent in the long tradition of just war theory—with the exception of Janna Thompson, whose position we will discuss in a moment). Accordingly, terrorists would be mere criminals, not combatants (not even criminal combatants, apparently).

Coates, therefore, does not understand why the killing of civilians by terrorists should fill a person with more loathing than the killing of soldiers or policemen. Indeed, he even thinks:

In normal circumstances a reverse reaction is discernible, the murder of policemen provoking greater not less moral outrage than the death of ordinary civilians.

And he concludes:

It seems, therefore, that if any criterion of war merits greater application to terrorism than any other, it is not "non-combatant immunity" (and not "just cause"), but the logically prior principle of legitimate authority.[2]

With this, it seems, we are already in the midst of the uncanny realm of double standards which I announced in the introduction. Coates does not offer us an explicit definition of "terrorism", but judging from what he is saying here, we are probably only dealing with terrorism if the violence in question is exercised by "illegitimate authorities". If Hamas—or better yet—if unorganized single fighters in the Gaza strip blow up an Israeli tank (which, according to international law and the laws of war, is a legitimate action against soldiers of an occupying power, or at least no war crime), it is terrorism; if Sharon, elected democratically, has helicopters fire into groups of Palestinian civilians (according to international law and the laws of war unequivocally a war crime), it is at once something completely different. (This linguistic usage is unfortunately also habitual with many of our so very objective journalists, at least in the USA and Germany—instead of consulting the PR handbook of the Israeli army they should perhaps better turn to the laws of war or a dictionary.)

One might object here that I am somewhat quick in making the reproach of double standards, for there could, perhaps, be good reasons for Coates' emphasis on legitimate authority. We shall investigate this in greater detail in what follows; at this point, however, it must be said that it is Coates who reaches his conclusion, cited above, too fast. First, he does not explain in what way the principle of legitimate authority should be "logically prior"; nor—what is more—does he explain how this principle is logically prior *with respect to* the principle of non-combatant immunity, as the quote implies.[3] ("Combatants" traditionally means "soldiers", but in more modern versions of just war theory their commanders and those who directly contribute to the war effort are also included, e.g. workers in munitions factories. We shall deal with this principle and its difficulties in detail further below.[4]) What could this possibly mean? Are we to take this to mean that the question as to who is a non-combatant and who is not—that is, who may justifiably be attacked and who may not—depends upon the view of the authority, which has the right to decide about the entry into war? If, therefore, the legitimate authority says: "I hereby declare that the children of our enemies are combatants; therefore, let us first bomb the kindergartens, the children's homes and clinics, for then our enemies will be demoralized and knuckle under", is that alright then? If this is in fact what is meant by "logical priority" (and I do not know what else could be meant by it), the whole just war theory collapses into an enabling act for "legitimate authorities".[5]

Second, if people "in normal circumstances" *really* should regard an attack on an armed soldier or policeman as more reprehensible than an attack on an unarmed civilian (which I strongly doubt), let alone an attack on (as one used to say) "defenceless women and children", this would not be so much a reason to abandon the central position of the principle of non-combatant immunity. Rather, it would probably give us good reason to recommend that those people work on their moral intuitions.

Does Coates have some further and, above all, some better reason to ascribe such a high value to the principle of legitimate authority? Well, at least he has an honourable reason, namely the prevention of wars. In this connection he appeals to Augustine, the father of the (Christian) tradition of just war theory:

"The natural order," he wrote in *Contra Faustum*, "which seeks the peace of mankind, ordains that the monarch should have the power of undertaking war if he thinks it advisable."

And he explains:

The widespread occurrence of private war was an urgent problem when the tradition was still in its infancy..., and it is hardly less of a problem today given the proliferation of self-constituted revolutionary movements and the common use of armed force or terror by non-state or sub-state agencies with an ideological proclivity to violence.... To insist on the public monopoly of the use of force remains a fundamental step in any process of pacification, and securing that monopoly is a precondition of civilized society.[6]

This depends on what one means by "civilized". If Louis XIV had succeeded in monopolizing the violence in his state, we might today be dealing with an absolutist French neighbour, with Louis XXI instead of with Jacques Chirac; and if the British had succeeded in enforcing the public monopoly of the use of force, the USA would perhaps still be a colony of Great Britain. To put it more generally: It may be that the public monopoly of violence is a precondition for a "civilized society", but *breaking* this monopoly of violence is a historical and, under most circumstances even today, an indispensable precondition for democratization.

Besides, Coates' one-sided intonation in the above quote veils the fact that the actual enforcement of public monopolies of force, while reducing the *number* of wars or violent conflicts, does not necessarily reduce the dimensions of violence taken as a whole. For there are not only subnational groups but also states which ascribe to themselves a historical mission and have an ideological proclivity to violence. In fact, the greatest crimes in human history have been committed by states or empires, not by subnational terror groups or guerrilla movements. Coates ignores this generally known fact and claims instead:

Modern revolutionary war is countervalue warfare in its purest form, a war directed against an entire society with all its attendant institutions (that is, instruments of repression and control). The likelihood of its remaining limited, therefore, is always remote, and its tendency to become total well-nigh irresistible.[7]

For this claim, which Coates makes repeatedly in one form or another, he offers no evidence. This is not surprising, for the claim is wrong and bespeaks conceptual confusion. First of all, it is quite difficult to wage war against values (one cannot shoot values, after all). Of course, Coates might use the term "countervalue warfare" here simply in the sense of deterrence theory, namely as contrasted with "counterforce warfare". The former would consist in targeting things that the other side values—mainly its population. However, not only is it empirically wrong that revolutionaries necessarily target the population, it is also empirically wrong that the governments that revolutionaries fight against necessarily value their population (most, in fact, do not; they value their armed forces, with which they repress the population, more by far). But perhaps Coates means that a revolutionary war is one that is supposed to replace an order in which certain values upon which the revolutionaries frown are institutionalized (e.g. despotism) by an order in which other values are institutionalized (e.g. democracy and human rights). (Incidentally, this is not a modern development, but a definitional property of revolutions.) The idea that such a revolutionary struggle necessarily degenerates into total war only becomes plausible if one conflates a state order with society, which Coates in fact does. The revolutionary movements in El Salvador and Nicaragua, for example, by no means fought against the society, but rather represented it; nor did they wage a total war—the governments did that (with the friendly support of the USA, self-proclaimed champion, with an ideological proclivity to violence, of anti-terrorism, democracy and human rights).

I should emphasize that Coates only confuses society and order or, as one may also put it, society and state at *this* point, for generally he does distinguish the two things. Yet this makes it even harder to understand how he comes to his extremely negative, indeed hostile, assessment of revolutionary movements.

For instance, he deplores the fact that for many "legitimate authority has become entirely subordinated to the concept of state sovereignty" because he sees in this subordination the reason for the diminishing influence of the criterion of legitimate authority regarding the question of legitimization of war.[8] According to Coates, the principle in its earlier and traditional form was far more demanding—which is incorrect, as in fact medieval theorists for the most part subsumed legitimate authority to the sovereignty of the ruler.[9] Be that as it may, the more demanding interpretation that Coates offers us reads as follows:

Legitimate authority is not to be taken for granted. The state's *right* to war derives not from its *de facto* or "coercive" sovereignty—that would be to accept the realist contention that international relations constitute a state of war—but from its membership of an international community to the common good of which the state is ordered and to the law of which it is subject.[10]

Indeed, he even explicitly turns against a too conservative interpretation of the principle[11] and explains:

A much more radical understanding of the principle is possible, and it is one that seems to be required by the just war tradition, given that the *vis coactiva* and the right of war is vested in the state as a political community and that powers are entrusted to rulers of governments as agents of that community. If that is so, the private appropriation of power by the government of a state undermines its legitimacy and establishes, at least in principle, the right of resistance.[12]

Even if one assumes, as Coates does, that legitimate violence, apart perhaps from in cases of self-defence, can always only be publicly legitimized violence, such polemics against revolutionary movements as his are still obviously inconsistent against the background of Coates' demands on legitimate authority. By admitting that state and society can oppose each other, he of course also admits that a revolutionary movement can *itself* be a public force, that is, force legitimized by the community. In other words (and with particular regard to the question of terrorism), if, for example, the community that stands behind the members of the Israeli army is a legitimate authority and can therefore make the Israeli soldiers agents and executives of public force, why should the community that stands behind the members of, say, Hamas not be such a legitimate authority, making the Hamas fighters the agents of publicly legitimized force?

This question is made acute by the fact that Coates, although he deplores the neglect of the principle of legitimate authority, does not for his part offer an even remotely clear criterion for when, precisely, an authority is legitimate. At any rate, he is careful not to commit the error, commonly made in democracies, of considering democracy as a kind of panacea:

[T]he power of even a liberal or constitutional democracy to resolve all problems of legitimacy is often greatly exaggerated .... Even a liberal democratic state, for example, is capable of serious discrimination against a minority ethnic community.[13]

With this, however, we are thrown back onto the two rather vague preceding quotes.[14] Taken together they roughly state that a legitimate authority is one which is a legitimate (whatever that may precisely mean) representative of a community and, in addition, one which abides by the law (whatever the law may actually be) that is valid for interstate or intercommunity relations.

With such an understanding of legitimate authority, however, Coates contradicts himself. Since he doubtlessly regards the requirements of *causa justa* and non-combatant immunity, which are (among others) necessary for the legitimization of war, as constituents of international law, legitimate authority is, against his claims, by no means logically prior in his conception, but rather dependent upon these requirements: an actor who enters armed conflicts without just cause and without respect for the principle of non-combatant immunity does not have legitimate authority.[15] Hence, the question of legitimate authority would be settled with reference to the criterion of non-combatant immunity, and Coates' criticism of the neglect of the former in favour of the latter would contradict his own previous statements.

In summary we may conclude that Coates' appeal to the criterion of legitimate authority does not succeed in demonstrating that revolutionary violence or terrorism (which, incidentally, is not necessarily revolutionary, and whose most frequent form is state terrorism) is illicit.

Janna Thompson, however, adopts Coates' approach and attempts to rescue it by introducing certain modifications. She discerns above all two difficulties in Coates' approach. I have already mentioned one: the criterion of legitimate authority becomes, in Coates' approach, dependent upon the criterion of just cause. The second difficulty consists in the implication of Coates' interpretation of legitimate authority "that states and organizations that are deemed to be fighting an unjust war—that is, violating the 'law'—have no legitimate authority, and presumably all their attacks . . . , military or non-military, count . . . as terrorist".[16] This is a conclusion which Thompson seeks to avoid. Her strategy in this regard is, to put it shortly, to define legitimate authority in such a way that its legitimacy is not undermined by only occasional violations of the law:

[A] belligerent must satisfy three conditions in order to count as a legitimate authority. First of all, it must be an organization in control of the violence of its members; it must be able and willing to enforce obedience to the restrictions of just war theory, to negotiate a peace and to keep it. Secondly, it must recognise (even if it does not always live up to) the restrictions of just war theory. . . . To this extent organizations that count as legitimate authority have to regard themselves as subject to law, though they may . . . not on all occasions be law abiding. But there is a third condition which also seems important. The leaders of the state or organization should be acting as the agents of its people [whereby "its people" is not necessarily to be understood ethnically, but in the sense of "the people in whose name or for whose sake it claims to act"].[17]

Violence which has not been legitimized by a legitimate authority in this sense (and which is not justified by strict self-defence, I presume, or is even that supposed to be terrorist?) is for Thompson terrorist violence.[18] Thompson claims that such a definition is "closer to the popular meaning of the term".[19] If one considers, however, that according to this definition, as she herself admits, "all of the violence of the Nazis, including violence against armed forces of the Allies"[20] and also all "uncoordinated violence of the oppressed"[21] is *terrorist* violence (even if the perpetrators of this violence scrupulously abide by *jus in bello*), one can only state that she is, in fact, miles away from what is normally understood as terrorism. To be sure, she made the former admission in an earlier article. Meanwhile, she has tried to escape this unpalatable implication of her view by saying that "a state or authority that is lawless in some of its affairs may be law abiding in respect to others" and that an "organization can be a legitimate authority in respect to some acts...and not [to] others."[22] The problem, however, is that her criteria of legitimacy quite simply still do have the completely counter-intuitive implication that all the violence of the Nazis, including violence against the armed forces of the Allies, was terrorist. Contrary to what she is trying to do, they do not allow for a relativization of legitimate authority to acts. Moreover, this attempt at relativization goes against the grain of her argument: it is not the character of the authority that determines here whether the act is terrorist, but the nature of the act that determines whether the authority is legitimate in respect of the act (whatever that might mean). In other words, "legitimate authority" no longer plays the role of a criterion here. Moreover, if such a relativization is allowed, why should it not also be allowed for subnational groups or single individuals? A subnational militant could be a legitimate authority with regard to some acts (buying milk, killing soldiers of an occupation force) and illegitimate with regard to others (blowing up school buses).

Thompson not only fails to solve the smaller problems in Coates' approach; its central difficulty, too, is only reproduced by her. I have stated that her admission that terrorism can be justified under certain circumstances makes her position inconsistent. While the principle of legitimate authority was, in Coates' argument, ultimately dependent upon the criteria of just cause and non-combatant immunity (and therefore superfluous), in Thompson's argument this criterion is (implicitly) even *rejected*. If, for instance, a revolutionary "campaign of terror directed against the perpetrators of injustice might be justified",[23] it logically follows from this, in the light of her definition of terrorism, that an armed campaign can be justified even *without* the allegedly so very important criterion of legitimate authority being fulfilled.

Of course, Thompson, like Coates, apparently only wishes to speak of a *warring* party if this party has been sent to war by a legitimate authority. One could, in addition, be tempted to claim that just *war* theory only applies to war, not to terrorism (which, for Coates and Thompson, is by definition not a form of war). If one tries to avoid the contradiction just described in this way, however, one restricts the scope of just war theory in a way which has certainly never been intended by its advocates (with the exception, perhaps, of Coates and Thompson). For the theory does claim to be the suitable yardstick for *all* wars (in the sense of normal usage, not in Coates' legitimistic one). In fact, Coates and Thompson themselves use this theory in their criticism of terrorism. How should that be (legitimately) possible if the theory is not applicable to terrorism?

Thompson's discussion of legitimate authority, then, is inconsistent. Nevertheless, we shall take a closer look at the criteria of legitimacy offered by her, as well as at the somewhat one-sided use she makes of them.

Thompson thinks that the suicide attacks committed by Palestinians in the Middle East are not compatible with the first of the conditions which she mentions. The attacks are therefore terrorist, for

[i]t seems doubtful that these acts were ever in the control of Yasser Arafat's government, and Israel will probably not be able to bring them to an end just by negotiating with Arafat.[24]

Yet she also believes:

A state which unjustly invades the territory of another isn't necessarily committing acts of terror by attacking and killing those who oppose it. Its aims may be limited.... Nor should a state be accused of terrorism just because it sometimes violates just in bello restrictions. Those who fight an unjust war or violate restrictions on war deserve condemnation. But the term "terrorist" should be reserved for those whose actions or ideological commitments show that they are truly outside of the law—at least in respect to some of their policies and actions—and have no intention of obeying reasonable restrictions.[25]

But in what way do the organizations which commit suicide attacks, or which have them committed, violate the first condition stated by Thompson? This condition only demands, after all, that legitimate authorities have the violence of their members under their control. This, however, is hardly less true of Hamas than of the Israeli army or the Israeli state. Of course, it may well be that *Arafat* did not control Hamas (indeed, this is even certainly so), but Arafat was, after all, no more the head of Hamas than Kofi Annan is the head of Israel. In other words, denying that the suicide attacks fulfilled the criterion of legitimate authority (and this precisely in Thompson's sense) because Arafat did not control them is like denying that the homicide attacks of the Israeli army or security services fulfil this criterion because Annan does not control them. To put it still differently: Thompson compares apples with oranges—which is quite common among Western critics of terrorism.

What about the second condition? According to this condition, in order to count as a warring party with legitimate authority one must recognize the restrictions of just war theory—but one need not always comply with them. Yet I do not see how Hamas—or, for that matter, the Palestine Liberation Organization (PLO)—recognizes the restrictions of just war theory less in words than Israel does. In fact, Hamas' deeds (let alone the deeds of the PLO) clash much less with this theory than do those of the state of Israel. Israel is the aggressor and occupier, the Palestinians are the defenders. Thus Israel does not fulfil the criterion of just cause and hence the one of right intention either—let alone the rule of proportionality. One could object that by not recognizing Israel's right to existence Hamas infringes the criterion of just cause, too. But that is wrong. And it is wrong not only because one may doubt the right to existence of a state with, for example, an exclusively "Jewish identity", a state which—in the view of those who have the say in that state, at least—apparently must refuse Palestinian refugees the right to return and expose the Arabic population to racist and nationalist discrimination. One could, after all, also imagine a multi-ethnic, Israeli-Palestinian liberal-democratic state with a multicultural attitude, instead of the present fear of racial contamination and emphasis on a Jewish *Leitkultur.* (To such a state, however, Hamas certainly does not aspire.) No, it is sufficient for the *causa justa* criterion just to *have* a just cause; whether one is motivated by it, or by it alone, is only significant for the criterion of right intention. Non-combatant immunity, in turn, is violated by both sides, but here Israel, measured against the dead it is responsible for, lies far ahead of the Palestinian side. In fact, few states have shown as clearly as Israel had even in the first years of its foundation "that they are truly outside of the law and have no intention of obeying reasonable restrictions". In any case, UN resolutions and international law mean nothing to this state, and human rights apparently only very little.

Perhaps Thompson would even agree with this appraisal of Israel; in any case, she does not explicitly defend Israel against the reproach of terrorism (the above quote on the state that unjustifiably invades foreign territory, however, does arouse the suspicion that she indeed has Israel or the USA or both in mind here). But this is not important at this point; rather, I should like to emphasize that just because an organization is subnational does not mean that it cannot fulfil the two Thompsonian conditions as well as states can. This also holds true for the third condition, as we shall see later.

First, however, I would like to point to a further problem ensuing from the second condition for Thompson's definition of terrorism. From this condition it follows that a state which fulfils the first and the third conditions can commit a terrorist act only if this state violates the restrictions of just war theory to some extent or, so to speak, habitually. For only in this way can it lose its legitimate authority. Thus one and the same course of action, for example the bombing of children's homes, is not yet an act of terrorist violence when it is pursued for the first or second time, but only, perhaps, when pursued a forty-third time. This, however, is more or less like telling a woman that she has not been raped because the perpetrator in question has only infringed the rule of consensual sexual intercourse for the first time, and that he is otherwise a law-abiding citizen. In this way *acts*—terrorist acts or rapes—are confused with *habits*. That is certainly not conducive to clarity, but it may very well lead to the obfuscation, and even the perpetuation, of crimes: "Don't worry; what happens for a first time is by far not such a terrible crime as it is when it happens for the fortieth time." This is a further reason to reject Thompson's strange definition of terrorism.

Let us turn to the third condition:

The leaders of the state or organization should be acting as agents of their people .... A group will count as terrorist if ... it is not the agent of the people in whose name or for whose sake it claims to act.[26]

Thompson explains that al-Qaeda, the Baader Meinhof gang and the Red Brigade do not fulfil the third condition, since these organizations do not represent the people in whose name or interest they claim (or claimed) to act.[27] If an actor, be it a subnational organization or a state, can no longer lay claim to legitimate authority as soon as it actually ceases to represent those it claims to represent, then not only the USA but also the organization known as the "United Nations" is in a bad position. For the latter claims, as is already clear by its name, to represent the nations of the world—and hence ultimately the world population. But this it does not do, for a large number of the alleged "representatives" sitting in the committees are by no means representatives of their nations, but at best representatives of their repressive upper class. What is more, some of its members are more equal than others; and these members tend to distort the results of decision processes within the UN in their favour. Thus, the "United Nations" does not fulfil the third Thompsonian condition. Blue helmet missions, accordingly, would be terrorism. As for the USA, it now claims to represent the "civilized world" in almost everything it does. That the latter regards itself as being particularly well represented by the USA one will be permitted to doubt. US military interventions are, therefore, terrorist acts. Inversely, it would seem that the leadership of Hamas does indeed represent its members, and that the organization as a whole does represent a considerable part of the population.

Hence, we may conclude that the "conservative bias"[28] Thompson quite correctly identifies in her position cannot even be upheld with her own interpretation of the criterion of legitimate authority. If one applies the same standard to each of the analyses, it becomes clear that subnational revolutionary organizations meet the criterion no worse than the adversaries of such revolutionary organizations—that is, states—do.

So far we have seen that those conservative conclusions which Coates and Thompson would like to derive from the principle of legitimate authority can by no means be derived from it. Moreover, both authors entangle themselves in contradictions in their interpretation of this principle. It is now time to ask why one should accept the principle of legitimate authority *at all.*

The core of this principle lies in the third condition stated by Thompson: One may only go to war with the permission of, or by the order of, a legitimate authority, and a *legitimate authority is, thus defined, an authority which represents others.* Thus, the decision to go to war can only be taken in a public function, and not as a private person.

This view betrays the provenance of the principle of legitimate authority from the Middle Ages, particularly its anti-individualist and collectivist prejudice. The idea that a single individual has the right to defend his or her rights against those who do not respect them and, if necessary, may do so with violence and against the state, and, moreover, that he or she has the right to violently punish rights violators, even if they appear in the form of a rights violating state, was alien in the Middle Ages—just as alien as the idea of individual rights. Medieval, too, is the considerable dose of metaphysics necessary for thinking that a community can have the right to punish, but that a single individual cannot have such a right. *Whence* can the community have such a right if it does not derive it from the individuals who come together to form the community? In contradistinction to the church fathers, the view of a *liberal* theorist such as John Locke is, in any case, that a community can only have the rights which its members transfer to it. There is no miraculous increase of rights by representation.

To this, no doubt, it will be objected that there are good pragmatic reasons to rule out private wars, namely in order to avoid wars. Coates warns:

As Aquinas observed, it would be very dangerous, for the community as well as for its rulers, if the overthrow of a tyrannical regime was left to the private judgement of individuals. To do so would be to invite social disorder and to render all states vulnerable to subversion irrespective of their merits.[29]

After a longer unsympathetic discussion of revolutions and revolutionaries, he then concludes the chapter on legitimate authority with the following result:

Faced with the very real threat of anarchy the norm that the principle of legitimate authority embodies needs to be very firmly upheld. As medieval thinkers realized, the key to all civilized living lies in the common acceptance of a self-denying ordinance regarding the use of force and a common recognition of its public monopoly.[30]

For medieval thinkers "civilized living" consisted perhaps not least in a situation in which authorities supposedly appointed by God told the subjects, at whose expense they were living, what to do and what not to do. That such thinkers should set the highest value on the principle of legitimate authority is perhaps due more to their own self-interest than to their care for the public. But, whatever the motivation of these anti-liberal thinkers might have been, the fact is that thinkers like Locke have a good answer to this conjuring up of an allegedly "very real threat of anarchy":

May the Commands then of a Prince be opposed? May he be resisted as often as any one shall find himself aggrieved, and but imagine he has not Right done him? This will unhinge and overturn all Polities, and instead of Government and Order, leave nothing but Anarchy and Confusion.

To this I answer: That Force is to be opposed to nothing, but to unjust and unlawful Force; whoever makes any opposition in any other Case, draws on himself a just Condemnation both from God and Man; and so no such Danger or Confusion will follow, as is often suggested.[31]

Incidentally, Coates can hardly reject this answer without inviting the reproach of applying a double standard. He explains that the state can function as a militant defender of international law and that it draws its legitimization to wage war precisely from this role as the defender of law.[32] He does not admit to the objection that nobody can be a judge (and, it must be added, an executing officer) of his own cause.

In requiring the state to be a judge in its own cause just war theory is doing no more than apply the basic requirement of any system of morality. The failure of states to act impartially, like the failure of individuals, is no reason for dispensing with the relevant moral code .... The decisions that are taken will inevitably be influenced by, if not always corresponding with, the prevailing moral culture, both national and international. States may well choose to violate prevailing moral norms for the sake of a national interest narrowly conceived; but given a wide enough and strong enough moral consensus they cannot continue to do so with moral or even political impunity.[33]

Thus, Coates gives the same answer to the suspicion of anarchy and chaos in the case of the state that militantly stands up for itself and international law as Locke does in the case of the individual who militantly stands up for himself or herself and natural law. If the answer holds good in the former case, it also holds good in the latter.[34]

   Contrary to just war theory, individuals—or more or less unorganized groups, for that matter—do not need the mediation of a representative (as in Catholicism) in order to gain legitimate authority for waging war; rather, they bear this authority themselves. If, under certain conditions, a *right to war* comes into operation, it is, or is based upon, an *individual right*.

With this, however, the criterion of legitimate authority is not completely refuted. Although it unjustifiably excludes private wars, for example wars waged by single individuals, it still makes good sense in regard to the question as to who within a community may and should decide about a "public" war, that is, a war that is waged by the community. One need not develop a theory of just war in order to recognize that it obviously will not do for a community as a whole to be involved in adventures by the decisions of some of its members, if these members have no jurisdiction within the community in respect to these adventures. For example, it would be inadmissible if the German chancellor independently decided whether the German armed forces were to be engaged in country X, because the formal authority for such decisions lies in the Bundestag. Nor is this formal authority sufficient by itself. Francisco de Vitoria already emphasized that the decision must not be taken without extensive deliberation, including discussion and the entertaining of advocates of contrary opinions.[35] As an example of application one may take the American president George W. Bush: The fact that he surrounded himself with (more or less eager) advocates of war, and (as one can see from his speeches) did not waste too many thoughts on dissident views; the fact that he refused to meet with American representatives of the church (all opponents of the war) in the run-up to the Iraq war, which he apparently ardently desired—all this manifestly excludes him as a legitimate authority.

2

Just Cause (Including Subcriteria) and Right Intention

As further criteria for *jus ad bellum* one usually finds *just cause* (*causa justa*), *last resort* (*ultima ratio*), *probability of success*, *proportionality* and *right intention* mentioned. If we understand just cause as only a necessary and not a sufficient reason for the permissibility of a war, all these criteria are logically independent of each other. For a just cause simply would not be sufficient. Although one might have a just cause, a war could still be illegitimate because of the non-fulfilment of the other criteria. Accordingly, the American Conference of Bishops, in its famous pastoral letter "The Challenge of Peace", declares:

War is permissibly [sic] only to confront "a real and certain danger", i.e., to protect innocent life, to preserve conditions necessary for decent human existence and to secure basic human rights.[1]

But why only then? Let us assume that the members of a war-games club are tired of shooting at each other with mere paint balls. They want to experience a real war. However, under no circumstances do they wish to kill innocents. They make their plan public on the Internet. Two million men, perhaps some women too, respond to their advertisement. They split into two groups, and each group buys land (the territories are adjacent); they establish themselves in their respective territories and agree that the group which conquers the other one's territory can keep it as a prize, together with the goods that are located there. Both groups then buy weapons in a race against each other; they train, and practise manoeuvres. Finally one group feels ready and enthusiastically attacks—and the others are happy that, at last, it has begun: the fulfilment of their dreams, a real war. This example is not as improbable as some may think. There are many who take part in armed conflict not least for the sake of adventure, the thrill. Be this example probable or improbable, what is important here is only what need be said with respect to the permissibility of such an undertaking. And it need be said that there is nothing wrong with such a war. If adults consensually decide to kill each other (and do not harm third parties thereby), this is, from a consistently liberal point of view, their right.

To be sure, one might object that the conflict in this example is not a war at all—the consensus between the parties is an obstacle to that. But it is not clear what role that should play. There is often consensus between the parties of a war on the *how* of warfare (*jus in bello*), so why should consensus on the *that* of warfare (*jus ad bellum*) disqualify a certain kind of conflict *qua* war? If the sides attack each other with machine guns, artillery, helicopter gunships and tanks, the conflict would seem to me to be a war, even if the parties have previously consensually agreed to such a measuring of power.

Let us consider a further example in which the rulers of country A steal all the domestic animals from the people of country B in order to abuse them in their own country as laboratory animals. As a result, country B attacks the thief country. B, however, has such superior weapons technology that it does not need to kill anybody; its ray guns stun the opposing soldiers (as well as some civilians, due to stray rays), disintegrating the weapons of the other side. There are, however, six casualties on the side of the victors, but all are soldiers (mostly former owners of domestic animals) who have volunteered. Victory is gained and the domestic animals are returned to their owners. Isn't this war clearly justified?

To most, it is too obvious that people may not do with each other whatever they consensually agree to do ("Where would we be if this were so?"); and thus they will hardly allow themselves to be convinced by my first example. Yet not only rule fetishism, but also the love of domestic animals, is deeply anchored in the hearts of many people, so that my second example may well be more convincing. Neither of the two examples, however, corresponds to the criterion named by the American bishops (in which "innocent life" means innocent *human* life). Thus, this criterion does not bear scrutiny.

A reply on behalf of the criterion which suggests itself is that in real wars as we know them today, not only are those who willingly assume the risks of war killed, but also many innocents and mere bystanders. Therefore, one might continue, the bishops are right, at least with respect to a real war: here one needs such strong reasons as they demand. Such a reply, however, misjudges the pretension of a criterion for just war. Such a criterion is, by definition, simply a criterion of *just war* (whether past, present, future or possible), and not merely the criterion of a just and more or less usual modern war.[2] Hence, the two examples do show that even a reason or cause which is rather weak in comparison to the reasons demanded by the bishops can be sufficient for the permissibility of a war if and only if the expected costs of the war (e.g. measured in terms of the death of innocents) are not too high in comparison to reasonable alternatives. But then it no longer makes sense to advance a catalogue of necessary reasons. Rather, the only logical and practical thing to do is to conceive of the criterion of just cause as a *sufficient* one (or rather as a nearly sufficient one, as we shall see in a moment), and hence to let it encompass the criteria of last resort, probability of success and proportionality.[3] Moreover, the criteria of last resort and probability of success, for their part, turn out to be subordinate to the criterion of proportionality, as we shall see.

Right intention, however, is indeed a separate criterion and remains independent of just cause (which is why just cause is only nearly sufficient). In its usual interpretation, this criterion stipulates that the *existence* of a just cause is not yet sufficient to legitimize war; rather, it stipulates that war be waged *for* this cause. If, for instance, genocide is committed in a country and stopping it is a just cause for military intervention, even considering the moral costs of the war, such an intervention would nevertheless be illegitimate if it were not carried out in order to prevent the genocide but rather in order to expand one's own sphere of influence. This is true even if the genocide is indeed prevented by the intervention. Judith Jarvis Thomson, however, considers it on principle to be a "very odd idea ... that a person's intentions play a role in fixing what he may or may not do". She adduces the following example:

Here is Alfred, whose wife is dying, and whose death he wishes to hasten. He buys a certain stuff, thinking it a poison and intending to give it to his wife to hasten her death. Unbeknownst to him, that stuff is the only existing cure for what ails his wife. Is it permissible for Alfred to give it to her? Surely yes. We cannot plausibly think that the fact that if he gives it to her he will give it to her to kill her means that he may not give it to her. (How could *his* having a bad intention make it impermissible for him to do what *she* needs for life?)[4]

Correspondingly, as one might say in applying Thomson's example to our problem, it is unclear why an intervention which saves a people from extermination should be foregone only because it will not be carried out *in order* to save the people from extermination. One might object that one would still behave *culpably*; but Thomson is well aware of this and it is not the issue here. The issue is whether the act is *admissible*. Yes, Alfred shows with his act that he is an evil man, but it would still be wrong to say that he ought not give the stuff to his wife, wouldn't it? Well, from the perspective of a judge the situation presents itself somewhat differently. Alfred's act simply constitutes the offence of attempted murder. And criminal law explicitly states that one *ought to refrain* from such actions. Our ordinary moral intuitions are in agreement with this. What, then, is correct? The confusion can be overcome if one distinguishes several things here. Giving the medicine to the woman in order to kill her is, it must be said, by no means the same type of action as giving the medicine to the woman without wanting to kill her.[5] Moreover, one has to distinguish between concrete actions on the one hand, and types of action on the other.[6] *This*, my drinking coffee on day *y* at time *x*, etc., is a concrete act; drinking coffee, in contrast, is a type of act. (Confusion, of course, is also caused by the fact that the word "act" can refer to concrete acts as well as to act types.) As soon as one has made this distinction, it is clear that the act type of giving one's wife a drug without seeking to kill her is permissible also for Alfred, but not the type of act in which one tries to kill one's wife. Alfred's concrete act, however, *is* an attempted murder. And attempted murder is *not* admissible. He indeed ought to have refrained from it. But the attempted murder saved her, after all! That was good, wasn't it? Correct, but these are two different kinds of things. One can say that it was *good*, particularly for the woman, *that* Alfred attempted to commit murder in this way (being a part of that force which seeks to do evil but produces good). Nevertheless, the attempted murder was *not permitted*; it was crime. The same is true of a concrete war. It may have been a *good and propitious* thing that it was waged, but as it was also defined by the intentions behind it, it is still prohibited, illegitimate and unjust. This also means, however, that there can be situations in which an unjust war is to be supported, but those who wage it are to be criticized for their dubious intentions.

It remains to inquire, of course, as to the conditions under which the intentions to wage war are dubious. Which intentions make a war illegitimate? In answering this question one must not think, as Coates puts it, "too puritanically".[7] It would certainly be exaggerated to say that a war may be waged *only* for a just cause. For instance, if an intervening power wishes to save a people from annihilation by intervention, this intervention does not become illegitimate by the mere fact that the intervening power also intends to expand its sphere of influence as a result of the intervention. Forbidding such accompanying intentions reminds us all too much of the Catholic injunction that one should only think of procreation during sexual intercourse, repressing all feelings of lust. On the other hand, the intervening power may in its war effort not go *further* than is necessary for the achievement of the war objective defined by the *causa justa*. Thus, if those military measures that lead to the intended expansion of the sphere of influence (or to the acquisition of resources) are necessary for achieving the intended just objective, there is nothing to be said against them. If they exceed what is necessary for it, this is inadmissible and the war becomes illegitimate.

We must once again repeat the question: May a legitimate war really only be waged *for* a just cause (although perhaps not *only* for it)? It is not on account of the Thomsonian objection already rejected that we return to this question, but on grounds of another consideration. Let us imagine a man who enjoys killing people. However, he respects the rights of others. Therefore, in order to kill people without violating their rights, he takes part in justified and legitimate military operations—and only in these. In such operations he does indeed kill those who are without exception legitimate military targets on the unjust side—but he does so out of the joy of killing, and not for the sake of the just cause. To many, such a person might seem despicable on account of his or her inclinations. However, having unattractive inclinations does not constitute a moral offence. One might find a person's paedophile inclinations repulsive, but one cannot morally blame him or her for them. One could only blame the person for acting these inclinations out. The joyful killer of our example acts out his inclinations, but not illegitimately. He respects other people's rights. And one cannot ask for anything more—as a liberal, in any case. Everything which exceeds this demand—and the criterion of right intention, as it is usually understood, goes far beyond it[8]—confuses moral judgement with snooping around in other people's attitudes and inclinations. It does not serve the protection of liberty and individual rights, but rather constitutes character surveillance. It has a totalitarian tendency, and hence there is every reason to reject it.

Our example is, of course, applicable not only to the single soldier or fighter, but also to states and organizations. A power that seeks to expand its sphere of influence by military means also acts legitimately if it regards this as admissible only in such cases in which it has the *causa justa* on its side, and proceeds accordingly. If, on the other hand, our said intervening power had also intervened when the condition of just cause had not been fulfilled, or had placed value on its fulfilment merely for PR purposes but not for moral reasons, the intervention would have been illegitimate. The legitimacy condition whose fulfilment is required by a well-understood—that is, liberally understood—criterion of right intention does not, therefore, consist in acting *for* the just cause but in *respecting* the criterion of just cause as a moral rule.

We now turn our attention to this criterion. Let us begin with the subcriterion of *last resort*. It would be exaggerated to interpret this criterion to the effect that one may not have recourse to the means of war before all other means are exhausted, as, obviously, one can always hold a further conference. Thus, one has to rather regard it as the last *promising* resort. If, for example, one wishes to save a people from a genocide that is already in progress, one cannot negotiate with the perpetrators for years, for then there will be no population left to save. Therefore, if time is pressing and it is foreseeable that nothing can be gained by negotiations and other means, but only by war, then the condition of last resort is fulfilled.

Even in this form, however, the criterion has to be rejected. It is *not* morally mandatory to use war only as a *last* resort. It can be preferable to other means in certain circumstances. A good example is economic sanctions.[9] According to the UN, the so-called economic sanctions against Iraq cost the lives of more than 500,000 civilians, mostly women and children. In war, the desired goal would have been reached with significantly fewer losses. To be sure, the sanctions were by no means economic but military measures, as reluctant as some may be to admit this fact. These sanctions were in fact nothing less than the traditional military tactic of siege. It was not rich owners of yachts who prevented the import of merchandise into Iraq, for instance by purchasing the merchandise from arriving ships at a price higher than that which the Iraqis could pay. (*That* would have been an economic sanction, but it would not have worked as a method for blocking exports.) It was rather *war*ships which forestalled the import and export of merchandise. That is a *military* measure. Nevertheless, if the sanctions really had been economic, for example if all non-Iraqis had decided neither to sell goods to, nor to buy goods from, Iraq, the consequences would have been just as catastrophic. In short, sometimes a war is the lesser evil, and this even if there are alternative means to reach the same goal (instead of not reaching it at all); for some means cause higher moral costs than a war, also and particularly in terms of human lives. Incidentally, it should also be pointed out that, under certain circumstances, it is inappropriate to declare oneself, in anticipation of a certain war against a country, against all forms of war against this country; for a concrete war (see the above remarks on concrete acts) involves a certain and *particular* way of warfare, with *certain and particular* costs. Just because, in a certain situation, a certain war against a certain country would be illegitimate does not mean that in this same situation a certain *different* war against this same country could not be even morally desirable.

The criterion of the *probability of success* says that a war is only just if it has a sufficiently high prospect of success, and this in the sense of a victory over, or repulsion of, the attacker. But with respect to self-defensive wars against genocides, this is obviously wrong. If the American cavalry in the Indian wars has surrounded a tribe and now wants to slaughter men, women and children, must these refrain from defence only because it is hopeless, that is, because it would by no means save them? Hardly. But even in a war of aggression, a certain prospect of success is not always necessary. Let us assume that a Native American people has already been strongly decimated by the army and knows that it can never resume its traditional way of life, but can at best vegetate on some reservation. If this people decides to set out for a last battle in order to attack its persecutors, despisers and oppressors, and to die together in this fight, then this is by no means reprehensible, or crazy, or fanatical; perhaps it is, as Barrie Paskins and Michael Dockrill memorably put it in a similar context, a "last flicker of humanity".[10] These are, of course, extreme examples of situations in which the prospect of success does not matter. Less extreme ones, however, can probably also be adduced. In any case, it must be said that the fulfilment of the condition of the prospect of success is not necessary for the justification of a war.[11]

The criteria of last resort and prospect of success are hence not independent, necessary conditions; they are merely, but nevertheless significantly, two points among others that have to be considered in the evaluation of *proportionality*. In order to assess the moral cost/utility ratio of a war, one must ascertain the prospects of success of the war, as well as those alternatives which are available and their (moral) costs.

On the other hand, particularly the costs of the war itself are to be clarified. This means, however, that the *jus ad bellum* is by no means logically independent of the *jus in bello*. If it is predictable that, under the circumstances given or to be expected, a war with a certain adversary will take forms that contradict just warfare, entering into the war will not be justified. But this is not to say that a single infringement of the rules of just warfare or, as we perhaps should rather say, morally admissible warfare, is sufficient to delegitimize the war as a whole. (At least one author claims precisely that.[12]) But if the extent and the gravity of the infringements are out of proportion with the positive effects which one could reasonably expect of the war, then the war is indeed unjust. Thus, the *jus ad bellum* criterion of proportionality does not, unlike the corresponding *jus in bello* criterion, demand proportionality from every single attack and move in war, but is connected to this criterion insofar as violations of the former can add up to a point where the war as a whole becomes disproportionate and, hence, on grounds of the said logical dependence, *there is no just cause* any more.

At the same time, one must not interpret the criterion of proportionality in a materialistic or "arithmetic" way. It certainly does matter how much material value is, on the one hand, destroyed in a war and, on the other hand, saved by precisely this "investment". In particular, it matters how many people, on the one hand, perish because of the war and how many, on the other hand, are preserved from death (e.g. when the war is an intervention against genocide). This matters because it is obviously morally relevant. Disproportionality occurs when the moral loss is greater than the moral gain. Some authors conclude from this that it is therefore also of significance which *values* are advanced or damaged by the war—be it by the example one sets, or by the witness one bears—and which moral *norms* one violates or observes, and to what extent.[13] With respect to norms a liberal can agree, but not with respect to values. For liberals it is not important to praise values or to bear witness to God, Providence or the spirit of world history, or to abide by their alleged commands; it is rather important that the rights and liberty of individuals are protected as much as possible. Here conflicts can arise, as we shall see in detail in the next chapter. For instance, in certain circumstances the rights of some can only be protected by violating the rights of others. Or it can so happen that individuals can defend their liberty only by risking their lives. In such cases questions of proportionality obviously emerge, for example questions as to how many human lives the liberty of the survivors is worth, or how many lives the renunciation of a defensive war against an invading army must save in order to compensate for the loss of liberty that is to be expected. On such questions liberals can also quarrel even among themselves, since the appraisals of the priorities may differ. The differences, however, will remain within certain limits.

Besides, it has just been stated that the principle of proportionality is connected to *jus in bello*. And of course one need not be a liberal in order to recognize the central norm of *jus in bello*, namely the requirement of discrimination between "innocents" and "non-innocents", or the principle of *non-combatant immunity*. The meaning, status and scope of this principle, it is true, are controversial. Depending on what the interpreters think of it, the answers to probably the most important question of war—"Whom may one kill in war?"—differ considerably. For they can range from "everyone" to "no one", and thus from always permitting to entirely prohibiting war—which apparently makes this principle the most weighty proportionality criterion. Precisely for this reason, a sharper determination of this principle suggests itself. This is promising because the different interpretations refer to a common pool of intuitions and principles, so that a rational analysis is possible here by checking the interpretations and theories for their consistency and their actual correspondence to our intuitions. Nevertheless, the further elucidation of the principle of proportionality shall only be a side effect of the following detailed analysis of the principle of non-combatant immunity. The said question obviously has its very own, dramatic weight and deserves a scrupulous examination in its own right: "Whom, if at all, may one kill in war (and why)?"

3

Innocents, Double Effect and Proportionality

I have so far used the two expressions "precept of the distinction between 'innocents' and 'non-innocents'" and "principle of non-combatant immunity" as if they were synonymous. However, the distinction between innocents and non-innocents is actually the original distinction in the tradition of just war theory; the equation of "innocent" with "non-combatant" and "non-innocent" with "combatant" is already an interpretation. It should be noted, however, that in just war theory the first and second pair of concepts are often used in a special, virtually technical sense, namely that of "illegitimate target" and "legitimate target"—regardless of the precise way in which legitimacy or illegitimacy, respectively, are evaluated.

But what, in fact, does the principle of the immunity of innocents and non-combatants, respectively, originally say? It *prohibits* attacking innocents with the *intention* of killing (or harming) them. It *permits*, however, carrying out military actions in which one *predicts* and *accepts* the death of innocents. An example may illustrate this. Consider a bomber pilot who has the intention to destroy a certain ammunition factory. He knows that in this attack innocents will also die (e.g. slave labourers or children who are for some reason present there), but their death is not his goal (perhaps he even deplores it); rather, he merely accepts it, since it is an inevitable *side effect* of the destruction of the factory. One cannot say that this pilot intends to cause the death of the innocents. If he were to learn later that the factory was destroyed by his attack but that, miraculously, no innocents lost their lives, he would judge their survival not as a partial failure of his mission (but perhaps even as a still greater success). Not so with the terror bomber. The Allies wanted to kill civilians with their bombardments of German cities; this was the immediate *purpose* of their attacks. They did not even make the attempt to hit military targets. Thus, they not only willingly accepted the death of civilians as a side effect in the pursuit of other goals, but they actually intended it. It is irrelevant here whether the death of the civilians was an *end in itself* for the attackers, or a *means* to achieve another end, for example the breaking of the morale of the civilian population. For one must necessarily *intend* both the ends and the means, it is claimed, while it is psychologically possible to merely accept side effects.

This distinction between *intended* killing, on the one hand, and *accepted* killing, on the other hand, goes hand, back to Thomas Aquinas' doctrine of double effect.

Nothing hinders one act from having two effects, only one of which is intended, while the other is beside the intention. Now moral acts take their species according to what is intended, and not according to what is beside the intention, since this is accidental .... Accordingly the act of self-defence may have two effects, one is the saving of one's life, the other is the slaying of the aggressor .... And yet, though proceeding from a good intention, an act may be rendered unlawful, if it be out of proportion to the end. Wherefore if a man, in self-defence, uses more than necessary violence, it will be unlawful.[1]

The last two sentences contain a principle of proportionality. Applied to war and the principle of non-combatant immunity, this means that one still cannot justify the slaughter of civilians by appealing to the doctrine of double effect—this, in any case, its advocates emphasize—provided only that one merely foresees the death of innocents instead of fully intending it (the word "accidentally" in the quote is thus inappropriate in this context). One may not bomb a kindergarten only because a recruit is in it at the moment. According to the doctrine of double effect as it is usually presented today, an act with certain predictable negative consequences is allowed when the following conditions are met:

1. The agent acts with a good intention, and attempts to bring about a good effect (or at least a morally permissible one).
2. The agent does not want to bring about the predicted negative consequences or side effects, and attempts to avoid or mitigate them as much as possible.
3. The agent treats the negative repercussions or side effects neither as ends in themselves, nor as means to another end.

4. There is an acceptable proportion between the predicted negative consequences and the positive effect.[2]

The doctrine of double effect is of essential importance in just war theory. Christianity was pacifist in character during the first centuries of its existence. But with the rise of the Church as a worldly power and the transformation of historical Christianity into a ruler's ideology, the church leaders saw themselves compelled (or were simply inclined) to justify the use of worldly violence. In view of the apparently pacifist teachings of Jesus Christ, nothing less seemed to be required than the squaring of the circle. From this come many rather contorted (though often quite imaginative) constructions in church doctrine. The doctrine of double effect is an example. This doctrine interprets, it would seem, the prohibition against killing in such a way as to maintain it while simultaneously allowing to kill.

Reactions to this move are quite varied, especially amongst proponents of the doctrine of just war, on the one hand, and amongst pacifists, on the other hand. The Christian philosopher and just war theorist, Elizabeth Anscombe, sees the virtues of this principle:

Christianity forbids a number of things as being bad in themselves. But if I am answerable for the foreseen consequences of an action or refusal, as much as for the action itself, then these prohibitions will break down. If someone innocent will die unless I do a wicked thing, then on this view I am his murderer in refusing: so all that is left to me is to weigh up evils. Here the theologian steps in with the principle of double effect and says: "No, you are no murderer, if the man's death was neither your aim nor your chosen means, and if you had to act in the way that led to it or else do something absolutely forbidden."[3]

A pacifist might, however, reply irritatedly—and in light of other statements by Anscombe, not without justification: "How charming! *Anscombe* is delighted about the conscience-easening power of the theological contradiction disposal service that generously offers one the opportunity to kill innocents while one is allegedly continuing to believe that killing the innocent is wrong—and then she has the nerve to claim that *pacifism* is guilty of 'universal forgetfulness of the law against killing the innocent'[4]!" To be fair, Anscombe clearly fought against abuses of the doctrine of double effect, for example Truman's attempt to justify dropping the atom bomb on Hiroshima and Nagasaki. Nevertheless, it is a sham to claim that the doctrine of double effect uncompromisingly affirms the absolute prohibition of killing. A prohibition of killing that is interpreted as it usually is in just war theory, namely under recourse to the doctrine of double effect, only prohibits the "intentional" killing of innocents, that is, insofar as killing innocents is what one means to do. The interpretation common in (contingent) pacifism, however, ignores this criterion, and forbids *any knowing* killing of innocents. To this it must be added that, in practice, it is very hard to determine exactly when a violation of the principle of double effect has occurred.[5] Whether someone intended to bring about a certain consequence, or simply risked it, is very often hard to determine on the basis of outward appearances (remember the "as much as possible" in the second condition above). One can thus often claim that one *did not* intend the negative consequences—and one is presumed innocent. Moreover, the principle of proportionality will be stretched as much as possible in the hands and mouths of generals, under the premise of "military necessity".

This is not a conclusive objection, of course. One does not have to allow politicians and the military to abuse the principle of proportionality. Just because they tend towards a rather uninhibited understanding of proportionality does not mean that one cannot hold them to a more restrictive understanding, or that they cannot be punished for overstepping these bounds through moral contempt, political pressure, legal sanctions (in the form of war crimes trials) or militant action. Besides, it is an oversimplification to see the doctrine of double effect only as a *danger* to innocents, for it also allows—as Anscombe points out in the quotation above—the use of "wicked things", for example military violence, in order to *save* innocents (as in the form of humanitarian intervention). It may be true that some innocents die in such actions, but the number of saved innocents may still be greater than the number of innocents killed. Pacifists are naturally ready to answer that saving innocents cannot justify the killing of other innocents, and they defend themselves against the reproach of being more interested in the salvation of their own souls than those of their fellow men—that they would idly (peacefully) watch as genocide was being committed—by explaining that killing is worse than allowing to die. But this principle is not clearly better than that of double effect; that intentional killing is worse than accepting foreseen casualties as side effects. Put another way: to argue that the doctrine of double effect is discredited by the fact that it makes some individuals less reluctant to kill innocents is precisely to assume what is to be proven.

We cannot, therefore, avoid examining the principle in detail. However, there seems to be a certain danger that, instead of finding sharp contours, the principle turns out to be somewhat blurred, to say the least. Jonathan Bennett, in any case, believes that no matter how it is formulated, the principle does not forbid the things one thinks it does. The prime example is that of the terror bomber. The terror bomber would have failed if no civilians died in his attack. He uses their deaths as a means to inspire shock and fear in the rest of the population, and to demoralize them. Thus terror bombing is forbidden under the doctrine of double effect. Bennett believes, however, that the bomber does not need to intend to kill civilians; in order to bring about the terror effect, all that is required is that the victims *appear* dead to the populace. If the terror bomber learns after his attack that the civilians had not died but, through some great miracle, were simply made "inoperative" long enough for their fellow citizens to believe they had died, and long enough to speed the war's end, he would not see his action as a failure. That such miracles do not actually occur, and that the bomber knows this, is, according to Bennett, irrelevant. Instead, Bennett attempts, as we have just seen, to get at the intention of the bomber by examining what he *would say, if* such a situation were to arise.[6] He concludes:

Of course the terror bomber knew that the people would become not merely inoperative for a while but downright dead—he had no hope of achieving the lesser thing without achieving the greater. But the greater thing is complex, and only one constituent in it was intended as a means.[7]

Bennett's argument impressed some philosophers so deeply that they looked for a "revision" of the principle of double effect.[8] At the centre of the debate was the third condition, as forbidding someone from using something bad as a means to an end seemed, thanks to Bennett, no longer enough to distinguish between tactical and terror bombing, and thereby to allow the one and forbid the other. This is, however, exactly what the proponents of the doctrine of double effect expect from the principle.

We need not consider here the proposals for revising the doctrine of double effect. In my view, the entire debate is misguided. The problem Bennett believes he has presented does not exist.[9] Even if the terror bomber intended the appearance that there were civilian deaths, it is simply false that this is *all* he intended. In the end, the terror bomber knows that, given the way the world works, the apparent deaths which are means to achieving the intended effect can themselves only be achieved by means of *killing*. We are dealing here with a causal chain that the bomber fully understands—as Bennett himself admits. The circumstances Bennett describes, that the terror bomber would *welcome* the miracle and not pursue the deaths of the civilians further if he could achieve the terror effect otherwise, show that he does not pursue the death of civilians as an *end in itself*, but not that he does not pursue this as a *means to an end*.[10] If someone *knows* that he can only achieve Y by doing X, and does X in the hope of achieving Y, this is nothing other than pursuing X as a means to Y.

Jeff McMahan believes, however, that the solution is not quite so simple:

It might ... be argued that the terror bomber must intend to kill the civilians as a means of making them appear dead, in which case the killings turn out to be intended after all. ... One problem with these responses is that they appear to exclude some applications of the DDE [Doctrine of Double Effect] that its proponents have wished to defend. ... Consider:
Self-Defence 1: One's only defence against an unjust and potentially lethal attack is to shoot the attacker at close range with a flame-thrower.
   The followers of Aquinas would accept that, in Self-Defence 1, it is possible to fire the flame-thrower intending only to incapacitate and not to kill the attacker, while foreseeing that one's action would in fact kill him in the process of incapacitating him. ... But, since it is plausible to suppose that the *killing* of the attacker need *not* be intended as a means of self-defence, it is therefore unlikely that one can show that the terror bomber must intend to kill the civilians by arguing either that the killing is a means of making them appear dead or that killing is too close to the intended effect to be itself unintended.[11]

A few things must be noted here. First, one can reply to the example of the flame-thrower with a similar, though differently intended, example and commentary from Philippa Foot. In this example, on the way out after a spelunking expedition, a fat man gets stuck in an opening, blocking the way for his companions. Unluckily, the water level in the cave begins to rise, such that everyone will drown if the opening cannot be cleared. The only possibility is to use some dynamite, which one of the spelunkers happens to have brought, and blow up the fat man. Foot suggests that it would be ludicrous for the spelunkers to argue that the death of the fat man was simply a predictable consequence of the explosion. ("We didn't want to kill him... only to blow him into small pieces."[12]) Foot is surely right in this suggestion. Can this be applied to the flame-thrower example? Well, if the flame-thrower creates a temperature such that a human target is instantly turned to ashes, it obviously can. It is simply nonsense to say: "I didn't want to kill him, just turn him into ashes." The situation would perhaps be different if we assume that the flame-thrower only burns the skin of the attacker such that he is unable to fight, and that he will only later succumb to his injuries. However, McMahan himself says that the man dies "in the *process* of incapacitating him", and thus not as a later consequence. Under *this* assumption, I see no difference between this example and that from Foot. Moreover, in this case, the death is clearly a means to bring about the incapacitation. If the incapacitation is first achieved when the attacker dies, then the attacker was incapacitated *by* being killed. (The converse would not be true, as death is sufficient for incapacitation, but incapacitation is not sufficient for death.) If, however, we assume for the sake of argument that the incapacitation occurs *before* death, then death obviously cannot be a means towards achieving incapacitation, as there is no such thing as "backward causation". On the other hand, the appearance of death in the terror bombing example occurs only *after*, or at least simultaneously with, the actual deaths. McMahan's flame-thrower example thus cannot refute the objection against Bennett.

In terms of the question of what is intended as a means, there is yet another complication. One could say that even in the case where *death* occurs only after incapacitation, and thus that death cannot be a means to the end of incapacitating the attacker, the *killing* of the attacker is nevertheless such a means. This is so because pulling the trigger on the flame-thrower *is* the killing of the attacker.[13] Bennett objects to this line of argument:

[I]t is shiningly clear that you can intend to do X without intending to do Y even if your X-ing is your Y-ing. His pulling of the trigger was his killing of his wife; he intended to pull the trigger; he did not intend to kill his wife.[14]

One can imagine here a married couple acting on a stage: the man believes (falsely) that his pistol is loaded with blanks and shoots at his wife. The situation is, however, not quite so "shiningly clear" when the man *knows* his gun is loaded with real bullets, and thus *foresees* that pulling the trigger will kill the woman. But let us consider the matter together with the question of means: assume that I give someone 10 metres away the sign to attack by wiggling my ears. I cannot—as I clearly know—wiggle my ears without moving the air around me. This concrete ear-wiggling *is* this concrete moving-the-air-around-me. Does that mean I gave the sign to attack by moving the air around me? Was the moving of the air the *means* I used to give the sign to attack? Obviously, we do not speak this way, and for good reason. Because even if the act with which I gave the sign was the *same* act with which I moved the air around me—so that in fact I gave the sign with the act that moved the air—we do not conceptualize *means* as concrete singular acts, but rather as (instruments and) *ways* of acting. And the way of acting that is described as moving the air is not identical to the way of acting that is described as moving my ears. In addition, we can not intend concrete singular actions. Holger's act of shooting Colin on such and such a date at 7 p.m. from a distance of 2 metres is a different act from that of shooting at 7 p.m. and 2 milliseconds from a distance of 2 metres, let alone from the act of shooting from a distance of 2.0000003 metres. Further variations can be found in the altitude of the gun: whether the gun is fired with the left or right hand; while sitting, standing or squatting; with pistol or revolver; with what calibre; etc. These conditions are *de facto* not specified to the last detail in intentions; nor would it be possible to do that. Thus one can only intend certain ways of acting; and thus one will never come to a level of specificity at which one's intentions are about a concrete singular act. In terms of the version of the flame-thrower example in which death occurs after incapacitation, this means that, while *this* concrete incapacitation may be identical with *this* killing, the defender *intended* neither this incapacitation nor this killing. Thus, since—understood as courses of action—incapacitating someone (even with a flame-thrower) is in no way identical with killing him (even with a flame-thrower), it does not follow that because the defender intended to incapacitate the attacker he also intended to kill him.

Another (supposed) difficulty is pointed out by Nancy Davis:

[A] doctor who removes a vital organ from a healthy patient to transplant it to another unhealthy patient has not brought about the death of the first as a means to saving the second. For it may be no part of the doctor's plan that the first patient should die from the surgery.[15]

This would be problematic because it is commonly assumed that the doctrine of double effect prohibits such actions. In addition, Davis sees in this example an indication "that there are some difficulties in interpreting the notions of means and end: these notions are neither straightforward nor unproblematic".[16] One should first note that, if the concept of means does not deliver what the doctrine of double effect requires, this would not suggest that the concept of means is unclear, but rather that the formulation of the doctrine of double effect suffers from an inherent confusion. Thus it must be said that, according to the interpretation of the word "means" defended here, which is in line with ordinary linguistic usage, the death of the first patient is in fact not a means to the survival of the other patient. Nevertheless, the first patient *himself* (and not his death) was used as a means, namely as a source of replacement parts (and the doctor's actions show that he or she understands this means–ends relation). Consequently, *using* the patient as a means is, in turn, a means towards the end of saving the other patient; and insofar as the use of a person as a means and not as an end in itself is wrong, something bad is intended here as a means to saving the other patient—which the doctrine of double effect forbids.

This ends our review of the supposed problems with the above formulation of the doctrine of double effect. The problems allegedly arising out of the imprecision of the concepts "means" and "intend as means" are purely fictional. Both concepts have a very clear sense:

- An instrument (drill, storeroom, etc.) or a way of acting X is a *means* of reaching an end Y when, under the conditions given in reality, X can be successfully applied (on the basis of corresponding causal relations) to achieve Y.

- X is *intended as a means* towards Y by a person A when A believes that X is a means in the defined sense, and A wants to use this means to achieve Y.

These concepts deliver, as can be seen, exactly what is necessary for the doctrine of double effect.

Now that we have clarified the meaning of the doctrine of double effect and shown the appropriateness of the formulation above, the following question arises: Is the doctrine of double effect correct?

Its central point is the distinction between foreseeing and accepting the risk of negative consequences, on the one hand, and intending bad means or ends, on the other hand. But is this distinction morally relevant? Some defenders of the doctrine invoke Kant for a positive answer to this question, as Kant argues that one should never consider people simply as means, but rather always also as ends in themselves.[17] As a defence of the moral relevance of this distinction, however, this does not help. It is extremely hard to comprehend in what way one is treating somebody as an end in himself, rather than using him as a means, when that person's death is considered an acceptable side effect or by-product of bringing about one's own goals. Why, for example, is it worse to run over somebody because you want his money (his death is here a means) than it is to run over somebody because braking would cause you to lose a race, thereby forfeiting some prize money (side effect)? Obviously there is no difference here.[18] Penal law sees it the same way: legally, both cases are instances of murder.

Naturally, *both* actions are immoral under the doctrine of double effect—and on the basis of conditions (1), (2) and (4). None of these conditions are met in these cases. However, these examples were concerned with condition (3), that is, with the presumed moral relevance of the distinction between side effects and means. It is enough to show *this* condition as misguided in order to refute the whole doctrine. But let us now consider a case in which the other three conditions are met. Let us assume that two virus-infected cats escape from a testing laboratory in the wilderness. If they are not killed before 6 p.m. on the very same day at the latest, the virus will escape out of the cats' bodies and, with time, kill millions of people. Two hunters are on the trail of the cats. A few seconds before six, the two hunters find themselves in two different quarries, in astonishingly similar situations. (Those who are familiar with philosophical examples will not, perhaps, be so astonished.) In each quarry, one of the cats sits in front of an old shack filled with dynamite. At the same moment, the demolition expert comes out of the shack carrying a vial of nitroglycerine. The cat jumps. There is, however, one difference between the two cases. Hunter A is close enough, and has a good enough shot, to hit the cat. He also knows, however, that his bullet will go through the cat, through the boards of the shack, and cause the shack to explode. The explosion will kill the demolition expert. Hunter B in the other quarry is too far from the cat, and knows he will not be able to hit the cat. In his despair, he comes upon the idea of killing the demolition expert (who presents a larger target), thereby causing the nitroglycerine to fall and explode. This explosion will kill the cat. Both hunters execute their respective plans and save millions of lives. Both have the best of intentions, regret the deaths of the respective demolition experts deeply (and maybe even of the cats) and act proportionately (the lives of one human and one cat versus the lives of a million humans). Conditions (1), (2) and (4) are thus met. Hunter A's case also meets condition (3), but hunter B's case does not. According to the doctrine of double effect, there is then a morally relevant distinction between the two cases, namely that A's act is permissible, but not B's.[19] This, I claim, represents a *reductio ad absurdum* of the doctrine of double effect. *That* is supposed to be a morally relevant distinction—that one hunter shot the demolition expert in order to blow up the cat, and the other knowingly blew up the demolition expert by shooting the cat. What would the demolition expert say to this fascinating distinction? Probably: "Dead is dead."

Let us consider another example from Nancy Davis. She contrasts two cases:

A doctor administers what she knows will be a lethal dose of an analgesic drug *d* to a patient who is in terrible pain. Any smaller dose will not be effective in relieving the pain. The doctor administers *d* intending thereby to ease the patient's pain, knowing (though regretting) that administering the drug will bring about the death of the patient.

and:

A doctor administers what she knows will be a lethal dose of an analgesic drug *d* to a patient who is in terrible pain. The patient's pain cannot be relieved without his dying: only if the patient dies will his pain cease. The doctor regrets the death of the patient, but she administers the lethal dose of *d* to the patient to bring about his death, and thereby relieve his pain .... According to defenders of the DDE, it may be permissible for the doctor in [the first case] to administer the drug, but it is impermissible for the doctor in [the second case] to do so .... But what can be the ground of *this* alleged asymmetry?[20]

This is a good question. A good answer from the defenders of double effect is, however, not to be had.

But aren't there other examples which do suggest the relevance of the distinction? Let us contrast the following two situations. In the first situation (S1), a hostage-taker has 100 hostages, and threatens to blow himself and the hostages up. The only possibility to stop him is to shoot him. Unfortunately, he is using Meyer as a shield. One must, then, shoot through Meyer, killing him (a side effect). A police sharpshooter does this on the orders of the mayor. In the other situation (S2), the hostage-taker has 99 hostages, and demands the death of Meyer, who is not among the hostages, but rather sitting, unsuspecting, at home. The only possibility of preventing the hostage-taker, who is this time protected behind thick, windowless walls, from blowing up the hostages is to kill Meyer (a means). A sharpshooter does so on the orders of the mayor. Intuitively, one would probably say that the killing of Meyer was morally allowed in the first case, but forbidden in the second. But does this really support the doctrine of double effect? A serious problem is the fact that these examples are about state power. The state may have commitments to its citizens that the citizens themselves do not have to one another. Philippa Foot, who presents a similar example, believes that we would denounce the action in the second situation even if it involved only private citizens.[21] Perhaps; though it seems to me that the condemnation would not be as strong then as it would be in the case of a state which kills its own citizens rather than fighting hostage-takers and blackmailers. In any case, the weakened condemnation, too, does not have much to do with the doctrine of double effect, as can be seen when we modify the example. Let us assume (S3) that the hostage-takers are sectarian believers in a variant of the Aztec religion. In particular, they believe that the sun can only be prevented from disappearing once and for all if, once a year, a person is sacrificed as "collateral damage", namely as the side effect of the killing of a chicken. (There are more peculiar religions than this one.) The Chicken-Aztecs obviously cannot perform the sacrifice themselves, because it is logically impossible *intentionally* to kill someone *unintentionally*. One can, however, intend that *someone else* kills unintentionally. The Chicken-Aztecs thus demand the death of a particular chicken, which they have carefully prepared so that the only method of killing it will necessarily also lead to the death of a person, in this case of Meyer. The Chicken-Aztecs have taken hostages in previous years with the goal of performing this sacrifice, but have not always been so successful with the positioning of the chicken: not in every case has the death of the chicken led to the death of a person. In the cases where the person did not die, the Chicken-Aztecs released their hostages, as promised, as they could hardly *demand* the death of the person, for if the blackmailed party complied with this demand, it would no longer kill him *unintentionally*. Thus, state officials and private persons, even if they know the intention behind the demand to kill the chicken, can still give in to the demand without intending Meyer's death as an unavoidable consequence. Nevertheless, in *this* case, the intuition—or at least, my intuition— also clearly speaks *against* the unintentional killing of Meyer. Whoever shares this intuition must allow that the decisive point in such hostage and extortion examples, which do at first glance seem to lend support to the doctrine of double effect, has, upon reflection, nothing to do with whether the death is a means or a side effect.

What, then, is the decisive point? It cannot be the fact that these cases involve extortion. Instead of 99 or 100 hostages, we could imagine just as many sick patients who can only be saved if Meyer is killed and his organs and blood plasma are split amongst the patients. Clearly, killing Meyer would not be allowed in this case. Where, then, does the distinction lie between this case (S4) and the first (S1), where the sharpshooter must shoot through Meyer in order to kill the hostage-taker? In my view, the moral intuitions in these cases can be explained through the interaction of *two* principles or rights. The first is the (not absolute) right to take action against attackers and threats. We will discuss this right and the objections against it in detail further below.[22] The second is the principle that certain individual interests cannot be sacrificed simply because such a sacrifice would serve the interests of many. This may sound at first somewhat "asocial", but it is actually nothing more than the basic premise of individual rights as such. Individual rights consist precisely in this "trump character", as Ronald Dworkin calls it, when opposed to the interests of a multitude. This does not mean that the strong interests of a great majority cannot also trump the right of an individual, but it does mean that some conditions would have to be met for it to do so. In the situation in which one can serve the interests of 100 people by killing 1, this principle certainly prohibits the killing. The individual right restricts the majority—this is the central principle of liberal democracy.

How can the stated differences in intuitive reactions to our examples be explained on the basis of these principles? In S4 the example deals with a conflict between the interests of 100 people in living and Meyer's individual right to life. It is important to note that Meyer's right to life does not conflict with the *rights* of 100 people to live, but simply with their *interest* in living. A person's right to life—at least, the so-called *negative* right, which is meant here, and which is more important than a possible positive one—simply requires others to *refrain* from interfering with this right (and thus it is a *negative*, as opposed to a positive, right). That is, it requires others not to do anything which would lead to the death of the person. One does not violate the right of a person who needs a kidney to live by withholding one's own kidney or that of another. This does not mean there is no positive right to life. It means, though, that this latter right is not broad enough to impose upon others a duty to sacrifice their own kidneys or those of others to someone who needs a new one. However, one violates (normally) someone's right to life when one kills him. (I say "normally" because, as mentioned, even this negative right is not absolute. One may, for instance, kill in self-defence. Self-*defence* is clearly different from self-*preservation.*) Because of this asymmetry in S4—Meyer's *right* to life, as opposed to the "simple" *interests* of the others in their survival—it is not permissible to kill Meyer. There would need to be an additional morally relevant element which would tip the scale in the other direction. This additional element is present in S1, in the form of the right to attack an aggressor. (By "aggressor" I mean an agent who is currently engaged in an illegal attack; or who has engaged in such an attack without having been punished since; or who is preparing an attack, gives the order for such, or intentionally and systematically supports one; or who has done one of these things in the past without having been punished for it since.) Meyer's right to life conflicts with a second right *and* with the interests of the 100. The conflict is clearly not in that Meyer's right to life *violates* another's right of attack, but rather in that it is *incompatible* with the other's right in this situation. As opposed to Meyer's and the 100 other people's (negative) rights to life in S4, Meyer's right to life and the sharpshooter's right to attack the aggressor in S1 cannot simultaneously be exercised. In the Chicken-Aztecs example (S3) and the example of Meyer's death as a means to saving the hostages (S2), however, the right to attack an aggressor is not pertinent. Thus we have the same asymmetry again. In short, in S1 killing Meyer is allowed not because his death would be a *side effect* of the attack on an aggressor, but rather because it is the side effect *of an attack on an aggressor.*

The explanation using the two principles is clearly only convincing insofar as the principles themselves are convincing. The principle of individual rights is hardly contested. Of course, one could ask if there isn't something irrational to it. Would it not raise the chances of survival of every individual if society decided to follow a norm like "When the sacrifice of an individual would save many lives, then the individual should be sacrificed"? In the end, it is logically more likely that one will be one of the many rather than one of the few. There are at least two problems here. First, it is not clear why, if one were to recognize such a norm, one should not recognize the more general norm: "If encroaching on the interests of an individual serves the interests of many, then this encroachment is allowed." This seems, however, to lead to an "absolute socialism", in which everyone must always serve others. This would, however, contradict the interests of *everyone* (excluding the occasional psychopath). Perhaps the aversion to the first norm can be explained by the idea that when one accepts it, one has entered upon a slippery slope.

Second, and more importantly, rejecting such a norm still would not be irrational, even if no fatal slippery slope were involved. Such a rejection would only be irrational if there were nothing more important than raising life expectancies. That, however, is not the case. A 20 year old who learns that having sex will shorten his life from 85 to 80 years would hardly be motivated to abstain. Another thing that most people would not sacrifice for life insurance is, without doubt, their *self-property.*[23] Without this, without having one's own person and body as property, one is not an individual, but rather a "distribual" or "social", ultimately a slave (even if only a slave on call). Note: *If* it is more important to somebody that he raise his life expectancy as much as possible, it may be perfectly rational for him to make a deal with like-minded people such that, should a clear case arise, the sacrifice of one or of a minority would be used to save a majority. All those, however—and this is presumably the majority—who find it more bearable to die of organ failure than to be one day, and in perfect health, picked up by some authorities and used as parts to save somebody else, should stay away from such contracts and reject the above-mentioned norm.[24] A person who believes in self-property, and understands himself as an individual with inviolable human dignity, places with good reason the principle of individual rights above the insurance of maximal life expectancy.

The importance of self-property and individual rights, in turn, explains the right to attack an aggressor. When an aggressor undertakes an attack on the life and limb of another, he violates that person's individual rights and self-property in the worst way. It seems then to be an analytic truth, one following directly from the concept of rights, that every *right* is accompanied by a corresponding further right to defend it.[25] And the more weighty the right, the more serious the measures used in defending it may be. Insofar as the protection of individual rights is hardly possible without attacking aggressors—some pacifists, of course, dispute this but, in my opinion, with little success—it is only reasonable to place great value on the right of attacking an aggressor if one also places great value on individual rights as such.

To avoid misunderstanding, I should make it clear that "attack" here, as the above examples show, is not meant metaphorically, but in its original, physical sense of a violent attack. If you hit someone or shoot at him, you attack him. If you insult someone, destroy his television set, or kill his child, you are not attacking him. Killing a person's child may be meant to get at him, but what gets him is the death of his child, not a violent attack. The child gets that.

This restriction of a (high-ranking) right to attack an aggressor to violent attacks is necessary. Let us consider a modified version of the case of the demolition expert. A spy and sharpshooter watches a meeting of high-ranking Nazis and Nazi arms developers through a telescope. They are out of range. A group of women, forced to do slave labour, pass between the spy and the Nazis carrying boxes full of nitroglycerine. A Nazi guard, also carrying a box of nitroglycerine, walks by, but the women are in the line of fire. The spy shoots one of the women in the correct assumption that she will drop the box and the high-ranking Nazis will be killed. (The slaves, however, also die in the explosion.) Compare that situation to this one. Instead of slaves, the wives of the Nazis pass by, and are not carrying nitroglycerine. The spy shoots them in the correct assumption that the high-ranking Nazis and arms developers will be so shocked and demoralized that they will no longer be able to pursue their destructive plans.

Intuitively, the spy's actions in the first scenario seem to me to be justified. Proponents of the doctrine of double effect, of course, see it differently—and we are not currently considering the pacifist view. But as an analogue to the original demolition expert example, we must ask why it is permissible to kill a slave by trying to shoot the nitroglycerine-carrying guard behind her, but not to shoot directly at the slave and kill the others as a side effect. The result is and remains the same.

In the second scenario, the situation is clearly different. Why does the second seem like an atrocity (and, as the pacifist would agree, certainly much more reprehensible than the first)? Well, for one thing, it is clear that the spy's assumption was not only risky, but downright outrageous. Of course it is *ex hypothesi* not outrageous in our thought experiment, but in such philosophical thought experiments it cannot be excluded that our ordinary expectations may, whether willingly or unwillingly, overshadow the predictability postulate of the example. In addition, our intuitions can also be explained through rule-utilitarian considerations. Because *even if* in this case the death of the wives broke the will of the Nazis, and thereby possibly brought a faster end to the war—and *if* this were somehow predictable—this is in most cases impossible, and thus drawing on such foreknowledge is simply un-founded and irresponsible. Precluding such irresponsible and fake justifications requires a rule which forbids *in general* psychological attacks by means of physical ones. (Of course, such a general prohib-ition is not an *absolute*—it could be trumped by a serious consider-ation of proportionality, or in the face of the unavailability of other promising means.) No less meaningful is a third aspect. John Locke argued that every individual in his original state—that is, before he gives certain rights to the society—has the right to punish an aggressor, meaning anyone who interferes with a natural right.[26] An element of this natural state remains in the right to self-defence, even in society. If the state cannot help an individual against an aggressor, he may help himself. It is true that in such cases one is to use only as much violence as is necessary to defend against the attack; but as soon as one defends oneself *offensively*, one has overstepped the bounds of *pure* self-defence. If, in one-on-one battle, a person does not just parry a blow but also reciprocates, then these return blows are delivered, on the one hand, with the goal of incapacitating the opponent and defending oneself, but on the other hand, they also—fully unavoidably and simultaneously—*punish* the opponent. This corresponds to the feeling one has while delivering such blows: one does so not just with pure defensive interest, but also with an interest in paying the attacker back. An attack on an aggressor, then, is not only justified by what the defender *needs* to do (in order to defend himself), but also by what the aggressor has *deserved*. Thus there is a double injustice in the attack on the Nazi aggressors by killing their wives. The wives die and thus suffer a fate they do not (we may assume) deserve, while the aggressors, the proper target of the attack, live on. It does not matter if the Nazis actually deserve to die. Decisive is, rather, that if *anyone* in that situation deserves it, then *they* do—but not their possibly politically uninvolved and misinformed wives. Although, in terms of what was achieved through their deaths, namely the military ineffectiveness of their husbands, the deaths of the women could perhaps seem proportional, their deaths nevertheless remains disproportional when seen from the angle just mentioned. And what people, compared to one another, deserve or do not deserve, and get or do not get, is a central aspect of our sense of justice.

The right to take action against threats and attackers and the concept of individual rights are thus plausible, and can easily explain any case which might at first glance seem to tell in favour of the doctrine of double effect. Thus there is no longer the least reason to continue to hold on to this doctrine, which, as we saw in our other examples, is itself anything but plausible.

Giving up the doctrine can also be recommended for moral reasons. The doctrine of double effect serves much more to ease the consciences of attackers than to ensure the well-being and rights of victims—and in this it belies its medieval origins. (These priorities are quite consistent in the framework of the Christian idea of life after death.[27]) "When you kill the innocent 'collaterally', that is you don't intend, but only anticipate, their deaths (but proceed anyway)," the perpetrators say, "then, assuming proportionality, it's okay." From the standpoint of the innocent targets and their rights, this may clearly be seen differently. One's right to life is no less violated by "collateral" killing than by direct killing. To contest this, at any rate, would seem extremely *ad hoc.* One could say just as well that being shot when the gun is held with the left hand violates the right to life, but not when the gun is in the right hand. One may object here that a different attitude is expressed in killing innocents intentionally as opposed to simply risking their deaths. That may be, but one has no *right* to be treated with a certain attitude or psychological disposition. The liberal concept of right leaves thoughts and feelings unaffected. The actions of individuals are merely restricted by the freedom of others. Thus, at least from a liberal view, there can be a right to life which corresponds to the duty of others not to kill, but no right to a kind of minimal emotional respect which corresponds to the duty of others not to kill happily (though they may kill regretfully). The right to life is, as explained previously, violated by collateral killing—and the benign wishes of the killer do not change anything about this fact.

This does not mean that it is morally completely irrelevant whether the perpetrator sees the death of his victim as unavoidable but acceptable, or actually intends to kill him. Of course this is relevant, and indeed relevant to the moral judgement of the perpetrator (but not, however, to the question of whether he violates the rights of the victim). This may be the reason why the doctrine of double effect seems plausible, at first, to so many. Obviously, they say, Aquinas did see an important point here. In fact, he did—but that which he saw correctly does not in any way tell in favour of the doctrine of double effect. The moral relevance of the distinction between intending and merely accepting a bad consequence of one's action is wrongly interpreted when one thinks it corresponds to the difference between means and ends, on the one hand, and side effects, on the other hand. Aquinas himself allows, in his famous writings on the right to self-defence, that one intends something bad, namely the death of a person, the attacker, in order to achieve something good, namely survival. (He allows this explicitly for agents of public enforcement, and does not, at least, seem to forbid private persons from intending and bringing about the death of attackers in order to protect an innocent, attacked third party.)[28] If, however, a public agent secures his survival by killing the other intentionally, his killing is clearly the *means* by which his own survival was secured.[29] What Aquinas actually forbids is simply that the defender be "led by personal passions".[30] He distinguishes, then, between sinful and sinless acts which aim at a good but also have negative consequences, and this not because the intentions and expectations behind the acts treat the negative consequence as means, in the one case, and as side effect, in the other case, but rather because of the emotional colouring of the intentions and expectations of the acts in question. In fact, it is *this* distinction that corresponds to the one between intending and merely accepting a negative consequence of one's action. Of a person who sees a certain means, such as the death of an innocent, as in itself bad, and who therefore on principle considers it only as an option of last resort, one can say that he only accepts, albeit reluctantly, the means in question. On the other hand, one can say of a person who sees the predictable side effects of an action as a positive bonus, that he intends them. In other words, the morally relevant difference here is not whether one sees the death of an innocent as a means or as a predictable side effect, but rather whether one welcomes the innocent's death or regrets it. However, the doctrine of double effect, as it is usually presented today, cannot do justice to this distinction.

The rejection of the doctrine of double effect has consequences. As we shall see later, one of these consequences is relevant to the evaluation of terrorism. The other one, of course, concerns the evaluation of war. For pacifists can rightly reply to philosophers like Anscombe (and to countless generals) that the doctrine of double effect is a lame excuse. If one simultaneously adheres to the absoluteness of the prohibition of killing innocents (the absoluteness of which Anscombe herself is convinced, after all), one has a cogent argument against war. The pacifist Robert L. Holmes puts it succinctly and precisely as follows:

Unless one can justify the actions necessary to waging war, he cannot justify the conduct of war and the pursuit of its objectives; and if he cannot do this, he cannot justify going to war.[31]

Since the condition cannot be fulfilled—in modern war, actions through which innocents are knowingly killed necessarily occur[32]— modern war cannot be justified. (Holmes leaves the question open as to whether medieval wars between armies of knights could have been justified or not.)

However, the argument has a blemish—namely its absolutism. Certainly, at first sight it does appear self-evident that intentionally killing innocents is absolutely prohibited. Anscombe even thinks that everyone who does not see this displays a "corrupt mind".[33] But one should not shrink from taking a second look, which shows that things are somewhat more complicated. Let us just assume that a madman can be prevented from releasing a virus that would kill all of mankind only by killing a certain person whose death he has demanded—would that be unjustified? Or would one rather be obliged to let the assassin kill all of mankind, including the person in question, than to kill this person oneself and to thereby save the rest of mankind? Hardly.

To be sure, Holmes concedes that, with the help of "highly speculative counterexamples", one can justify "war and killing of all sorts", and that for this reason he did not intend to advocate an absolutist prohibition of the killing of innocents.[34] This, however, seems more like lip-service if one considers how he deals with less speculative lines of reasoning. He adduces this one:

The reasoning goes like this: killing innocent persons in wartime is terrible and can be justified by one and only one consideration, and that is that sometimes it is the only way to prevent other innocent persons—perhaps in greater numbers—from being killed. As terrible as the casualties to innocents were in World War II, if Germany had not been stopped, many times that number would have died at the hands of the Nazis.[35]

In reference to this argument he concludes:

Two assumptions are central here: the first holds that there is no moral distinction between ... killing and letting die ...; the second holds that the consequence of refusing to fight is that innocents will be killed by the aggressor.... And you are, it is held, as responsible for deaths you could have prevented as for those you cause yourself.[36]

Holmes disputes both assumptions and deems that, in this way, he is able to invalidate the reasoning cited.

In order to refute the second assumption, he distinguishes unmediated from mediated consequences. Consequences are unmediated if they result from my actions on grounds of natural laws alone, without the interference of other people's decisions. Accordingly, consequences are mediated if they are partly dependent on other people's decisions.[37] If a pacifist nation B does not stop an aggressor nation A by war, though nation A is committing genocide, the consequence of B's decision to abstain from war, namely the death of the victims of the genocide, is mediated—without the decisions and deeds of nation A they would not occur. The death of the victims, however, is an unmediated consequence of the extermination measures of the perpetrator nation A. Holmes claims that it is not a factual but a moral question whether the mediated consequences of the act of an actor are indeed the consequences of his way of acting.[38] But that is simply wrong.[39] Whether an event is a consequence of my act or not is a purely factual question, namely the question as to whether my act belongs to the causal factors that have produced the event. Whether the other factors are atoms, pears, apples or the actions or decisions of other people is irrelevant. To be sure, one could perhaps argue with some justification that acts of *omission* cannot easily be understood as causal factors. If Fritz closed the roof window 10 minutes ago and I omitted opening it 5 minutes ago and now the rain bounces off the window, Fritz's closing of the window is a cause for the fact that it does not rain into the room, but my omission, so it seems, is no cause. In order to be a cause, a thing or an event X must *effect* something. And effects, so one might say, can only come from positive forces, from things that do or make something (therefore the expression "factor"), not of omissions and "failings". However, even if this were correct and omissions did not actually effect something (apart from the cases in which another individual reacts directly to the omission), they nevertheless still *make* certain things *possible*. In the example with the window I made it possible for Fritz's act to effect the room's remaining dry. But that which occurs because I have made it possible by my act of omission is no less a consequence of this act of omission than what I effected by a positive act. It is also unclear why one should bear no responsibility at all for the predicted consequences of one's acts only because these are mediated. In my view, one can safely put this pacifist doctrine of the double mediated effect into the same corner as the bellicist doctrine of double effect. Whichever doctrine one aims this criticism at: one always hits the right one.[40]

Besides, Holmes is obviously getting things backwards. In order to determine whether a person is responsible for an event (e.g. the death of an innocent), one *first* has to determine whether this event is a consequence of the act (of omission) of the person in question. If this is not the case, the person is not responsible. (If it is the case, the person is not yet automatically responsible; for example, the result may not have been predictable for him.) How could one possibly proceed in reverse? How could it be possible to decide on the guilt or innocence of a defendant with respect to a certain result *before* having clarified whether the actions of the defendant in fact led to this result? Besides, in his language, Holmes implicitly concedes that one can determine who has (partly) caused a certain event without having recourse to a moral assessment.[41] Whether a (partial) causation is to be morally condemned (not every partial causation of a bad event is to be morally condemned)[42] is another question, and should not be confused with the first one. Rather, it presupposes, as has been stated, that the first one is answered.

Regarding the first assumption, one may consider the following two situations. Situation 1: Ede's father breaks down with a heart attack in the presence of his son, who longingly awaits his inheritance. Lying on the ground, the father reaches out with his hand for some life-saving medicine. His son moves it beyond reach and watches his father die. Situation 2: Ede's father breaks down with a heart attack in the presence of his son, who longingly awaits the inheritance. Lying on the ground, he reaches out with his hand for some life-saving medicine. It is already beyond reach, his son leaves it there and watches his father die. (The death of the father, incidentally, is a good example for the consequence of an act of omission.) Some see here indeed a morally relevant difference. Others, myself amongst them, do not. That there is a difference is, in any case, anything but obvious.[43] Therefore, a pacifist position that needs to appeal to this alleged difference is very shaky.

Moreover, the two assumptions are *not necessary at all* for the reasoning Holmes criticizes. Raymond Belliotti points out in his criticism of Holmes that the said reasoning does not need a special sense of "consequence", for it relies merely upon what happens if nation B does not attack nation A, and on what happens if it does.[44] Furthermore, it does not require any position with regard to the *general* distinction between killing and letting die.

Instead, the argument from prevention takes a much more localized position on the relationship between killing and letting: the knowing and foreseen killing of a certain number of innocent persons within an aggressor nation in wartime, when there are no less horrible means of prevention available, is morally preferable to permitting that aggressor nation to kill straightaway a larger number of innocent persons in the nonaggressor nation.[45]

But Holmes thinks:

> Human beings have as much right to be spared destruction by good people as by bad. . . . If I choose to kill innocent persons in order to prevent the deaths of others at the hands of an aggressor, I, no less than and perhaps even more than he (if his killing of innocents is only incidental to his attaining his ends) am using innocent persons as a means to an end. If this is correct, the presumption against killing innocents is not defeated by this reasoning.[46]

Well, this is not correct. We have already seen that it is morally irrelevant whether one makes corpses of innocents in the pursuit of one's ends as a means to one's ends, or one kills innocents as a side effect of the pursuit of one's ends. Besides, it is not even true that the defender uses the innocents he kills as a means for saving other innocents. Their death is clearly a side effect.[47]

The decisive point, however, is that Holmes does not at all deal with the problem of *numbers* (the defender kills innocents and saves thereby a much higher number of innocents). He even admits this himself:

> It should also be noted, finally, that I have not taken up directly the many possible utilitarian arguments that might be given for war and the killing of innocents. ... This is because I am convinced that if the analysis of consequences in sections VII and VIII of this chapter are correct, it means that utilitarianism (and consequentialism generally) is inadequate as a basis for moral theory. I have not tried to detail this, but I believe it can be shown insofar as such theories presuppose that it is possible to make an antecedently non-moral determination of consequences as a basis for making moral judgments.[48]

We just saw that such a "nonmoral determination" is the precondition for the "moral determination", and that the fulfilment of this precondition is quite possible. Thus, his analysis of the concept of consequences is wrong. Even if it were correct, this would not hinder one from imputing to a pacifist nation the death of one million innocents as a consequence of its acts (of omission) if it should let these innocents die at the hands of an aggressor state because it is not ready to take the responsibility for the killing of 10,000 innocents in the course of a military attack on the aggressor nation that would save one million lives. Pacifists do not have a monopoly on the ascription of consequences. The appeal to the distinction between killing and letting die does not serve here, either, as we have already seen, for even if this distinction were morally relevant and killing were worse than letting die, this difference could still be trumped by the exponentially higher number of those one would let die if one abstained from killing. By rejecting utilitarian considerations—that is, the significance of numbers, the significance of weighing the killing of innocents against letting many more innocents die—as irrelevant, Holmes does turn out to be an absolutist. Insofar as the rejection of such weighing consider-ations is implausible and does not do justice to moral reality, in which there are dilemmas of the kind mentioned, dilemmas which cannot simply be made to go away by a *fiat* in favour of the alleged absolute priority of the prohibition to kill innocents, it turns out that absolutism is inadequate as a basis for moral judgement.

With the last two sentences, pacifism has by no means already been repudiated in favour of just war theory. Rather, what has been said here so far stands contrary to both theories. For just war theory assumes that a soldier who kills innocents under observance of the conditions stated by the doctrine of double effect does not make himself guilty. This view is to be rejected. It is not possible, either, to save the innocence of a soldier who kills innocents by pointing to the importance of the relation between killed and saved innocents. The utilitarian principle was not introduced here as a kind of functional equivalent to the doctrine of double effect. Observing the conditions stated by the doctrine of double effect fails to bring the result that killing an innocent is not a violation of his right to life. Yet, the same is true of the fact that the attack on an aggressor (or even the direct attack on an innocent) saves many other innocents. It also fails to bring the result that the killing of an innocent in the course of this attack does not violate his right to life. Therefore, I deliberately spoke of a dilemma—whatever one does, it is the wrong thing.[49]

Since there will not be a modern war without the killing of innocents (this much must be granted Holmes), no modern war can ever be *just.* This does not, however, preclude the possibility that a modern war can be *justified*—namely as the lesser evil.[50] This distinction is not a hair-splitting one, but rather one which is very significant for the purposes of practice. For the insight that a war, however noble its aims may be, is always an evil thing, and that those who participate in, or support, it make themselves guilty, leads away from a self-complacent heroic and moral triumphalism and to a more modest and reflexive attitude, one which is more appropriate to the tragedy that is war, and which can help to progressively restrict the dimensions of its evils.[51] But since, as I have said, this poses a dilemma, absolutist pacifists also have no special reason to pat themselves on the back for an allegedly superior morality. Neither can soldiers and their commanders wash their hands of the deaths of the "collaterally" killed innocents (they can at best wash them in the blood of innocents), nor can pacifists do this with regard to the innocents they let die. (Whose guilt is greater can only be decided under consideration of the facts of each concrete case, and not *in abstracto.*) From this it follows, in turn, that one has to take the dilemma by *both* horns—without the prospect of getting a firm grip on it right from the start. In other words, the increasing restriction of evil cannot consist in a unilateral abstention from war, or in acquiring an imperturbable peacefulness. Imperturbable peacefulness may be an appropriate virtue for sheep, but not for human beings. For only under certain circumstances is non-violence a functioning tactic to resist an aggressor and to cause his aggression to break down (e.g. in India against the British); under other circumstances, it certainly is not (e.g. in Germany against the Nazis). In order to increasingly diminish the evil, one therefore must, where this is necessary and justified in the light of proportionality considerations, stand up to an aggressor with violence. At the same time, one must acknowledge that the rights of those innocents who die through this counter-violence are indeed violated. This imposes on those waging the war the obligation to minimize these rights violations as much as possible—even if this means increasing risks to their own lives. It also imposes on them the obligation to grant "reparation" payments and support to those whose rights have been violated and their relatives.

The answer to the question put above—"Whom, if anyone at all, may one kill in war?"—is thus, at this point, as follows. Innocents have a right not to be killed by an attack, but not an *absolute* one which could not be trumped by proportionality considerations and the possibly conflicting right of another to attack an aggressor. This answer does *not*, however, clear the way for a justification of terror bombardments like the ones against Hamburg and Dresden. For one thing, such acts actually fail to fulfil the conditions of proportionality. I have already answered to the objection that the proportionality principle is vague and turns, in the hands of generals, into an excuse for killing innocents.[52] An absolute prohibition on the killing of innocents obviously protects innocents from being killed by adherents to this principle, but it does not protect them from being killed by those who do not adhere to it. Rather, it protects the latter. In this way, it only leads to more innocent victims instead of less. For another thing, it should be recalled that we have argued here for trumping the right of innocents to life not by an appeal to a mere principle of proportionality, but by an appeal to the combination of this principle with the right to attack an aggressor. This, in turn, has moderating consequences, as we have seen.[53] The immunity of innocents, although not absolute, is and remains an enormously important principle.

The rejection of absolutism thus presents us with, for the time being, only the following answer to the said question: "It depends." Obviously the answer depends, in particular, on the further question as to who then actually counts as an *innocent*. This will be examined in what follows. It will also become apparent that we have not yet finished our discussion of pacifism.

4

Non-combatant Immunity and the Definition of Non-innocence and Innocence

How are "non-innocence" and "innocence", respectively, to be understood in the context of wars and armed struggle? How exactly is it to be determined who is a legitimate target and who is not? In order to clarify this we shall discuss the most important approaches to these questions.

Let us here, too, begin with Elizabeth Anscombe. We have seen that she rejects direct attacks upon the innocent, that is, those attacks which are not covered by the principle of double effect, as absolutely forbidden. *Non-innocents*, however, may be attacked directly. She explains:

Innocence is a legal notion; but here, the accused is not pronounced guilty under an existing code of law, under which he has been tried by an impartial judge, and therefore made the target of attack. . . . This, however, does not mean that the notion of innocence fails in this situation. What is required, for the people attacked to be non-innocent in the relevant sense, is that they should themselves be engaged in an objectively unjust proceeding which the attacker has the right to make his concern; or—the commonest case—should be unjustly attacking him. Then he can attack them with a view to stopping them; and also their supply lines and armament factories. But people whose mere existence and activity supporting existence by growing crops, making clothes, etc. constitute an impediment to him—such people are innocent and it is murderous to attack them.[1]

Her distinction between the innocent and the non-innocent corresponds to that between non-combatants or just combatants on the one hand and unjust combatants on the other; roughly, between those who do not fight or who fight justly, and those who fight unjustly. Like other Anscombe-interpreters,[2] I am not sure whether she realizes that this way of making the distinction—if it is not combined with the often conceded overall excuse (which we shall discuss below) of soldiers for infringements on the *jus ad bellum*— deviates drastically from the laws of war, which do *not* consider the killing of just combatants (i.e. of combatants who wage a just war with permitted means) by soldiers of the opposing side as murderous. Innocents in the sense of Anscombe's characterization are not yet illegitimate targets, at least according to the laws of war. Since she says nothing on this point, although the deviation would doubtlessly have been worth comment, it is safe to assume that she did not realize it. Be that as it may, the correspondence mentioned above is "rough" because it is, as I have previously indicated, not always entirely clear who counts as a combatant, and why. An influential attempt at clarifying this is provided by Jeffrie G. Murphy:

> Combatants are those anywhere within the *chain of command or responsi-bility*—from bottom to top.... The links of the chain (like the links between motives and actions) are held together logically and not merely causally, i.e. all held together, in this case, under the notion of who it is that is *engaged in an attempt* to destroy you. The farmer qua farmer is, like the general, performing actions which are causally necessary for your destruction; but, unlike the general, he is not necessarily engaged in an attempt to destroy you.... The farmer's role bears a contingent connection to the war effort whereas the general's role bears a necessary connection to the war effort.... The farmer is aiding the soldier qua human being whereas the general is aiding the soldier qua soldier or fighting man.[3]

From this it follows that not only those fighting in the strict sense—those firing upon the enemy or carrying weapons in order to do so—may be attacked, but also those giving orders, presidents and ministers included. This view is supported by the laws of war.

However, this formulation is, as many critics have pointed out, not nearly as unproblematic and plausible as it may first appear. To use an example from George I. Mavrodes: a farmer could be a well-educated and fanatic supporter of the Nazis and their war who, while watching over his farm, saves every penny in the hopes of profiting from the Nazis' victory, who lends his voice to Nazi propaganda, and who does all this in the full knowledge of who the Nazis are and what they do (perhaps he has relatives working in the concentration camps or with the Gestapo). Conversely, an uneducated and naive young man who knows little of what happens outside his village and nothing of what the war is about could nevertheless be drafted to serve in the war effort, though he detests the service and wishes nothing more than to be allowed to leave.

But he is "engaged", carrying ammunition, perhaps, stringing telephone wire or even banging away ineffectually with his rifle. He is without doubt a combatant, and "guilty", a fit subject for intentional slaughter. Is it not clear that "innocence", as used here, leaves out entirely all of the relevant moral considerations—that it has no moral content at all?[4]

As this example shows, a civilian—an alleged "non-combatant"—may support soldiers qua soldiers and deliberately support the war and engage in an effort to destroy the enemy at least as much as do the soldiers themselves. Moreover, the farmer, in his support of the war effort, is obviously much *guiltier* in the moral sense than the villager. It is hard to assign much blame to the villager. Not so to the farmer.

From this Mavrodes does not conclude that the immunity of non-combatants is further undermined by this example, a kind of immunity which is already relativized by the acceptance of "collateral damage"; rather, he concludes that non-combatant immunity must be interpreted differently—namely as a useful *convention*.[5] The convention restricts the brutality of war in the interests of the warring parties. The fact that it is simply a convention does not mean that one need not abide by it. It is a convention in Germany to drive on the right-hand side of the road. Although it is not *in itself* moral to drive on the right (Australians are not immoral for driving on the left), it would indeed be immoral to drive on the left in Germany *because of* this convention (for this might cause many fatal accidents). It is thus a convention-dependent obligation, but no less obligatory on that account. According to Mavrodes, the same is true of the principle of immunity for non-combatants.

The claim that this principle is a simple convention is often disputed. Richard Norman, for example, points out that Mavrodes also discusses the idea of a single-combat convention: the leaders of the warring nations would settle their differences in single combat. Such a convention would obviously further restrict the damage caused by war. Mavrodes himself admits that there is no chance of such a convention being adopted. Norman would like to know why not, and suggests, of course, that the principle of civilian immunity is adopted because it does have convention-independent relevance.[6] However, one should not forget that war damage is not to be avoided *at any price*. Many find at least some things valuable enough to risk some degree of destruction. Mavrodes himself does not see this point clearly enough, since he describes the single-combat convention as attractive (though utopian). Yet the idea that, in a clash that would normally have led to war, "whatever territory, influence, or other price would have been sought in the war"[7] should instead, on the basis of this new convention, simply be handed over to the winner of individual combat is not particularly attractive. What if the winning nation is out to rape, enslave or murder the population of the other country? If one nation says to the other, "We'd like to commit genocide on your population", should the matter be settled by arm wrestling? Should the losing country then say, "OK, go ahead" with sportsmanlike resignation? If the war is not over genocide or enslavement but rather over "merely" a considerable restriction of freedom, is it honourable and *moral* simply to give up because one lost the arm-wrestling match rather than to defend one's freedom with much stronger means and efforts? (This would also be the argument of many pacifists who, rather than simply giving up for the sake of peace, advocate resistance by means which, while non-violent, nevertheless entail great sacrifice and loss.[8]) In short, the idea that the immunity of non-combatants is justified by its being a useful convention cannot be dispensed with simply by pointing out that the single-combat convention could have been chosen—because the latter just *isn't* useful. But if—one might object—it comes down to defending yourself against certain unjust and unbearable consequences with everything you have got, why should the immunity of non-combatants not be thrown out as well? It is perhaps useful to consider the comparison with "fighting honourably" or "fighting like a man"—concepts we know not just from Westerns but perhaps also from the school playground (or even from personal experience), whereby one gives the other "a knuckle sandwich", as they say, but avoids more sensitive body parts. The analogous question here is: if one is prepared to break the other's nose, and to risk having one's own nose broken, why does this preparedness not extend to other parts? The answer is obvious. In a fight to defend or assert one's manhood, it would be counterproductive to allow that which is being defended to be hit and perhaps permanently damaged. He who fights to prove he is a man would still like to be one after the fight is over. In addition, the chances of resuming normal relations after the fight may well depend on neither party suffering lasting damage. Such concerns provide men who become involved in fights with good reason to adhere to rules against low blows, and to consider such conventions a matter of honour. (If I understand correctly, such codes exist even among hooligans.) These considerations can be applied to the case of war between nations. A battle to defend freedom and self-determination would be undermined if it involved damaging the nation's most valuable asset—its capacity to reconstruct itself after the war. As Michael Green formulates it:

[N]ations will wish to limit war so that the possibility of their nation being totally destroyed is minimised, or at least significantly reduced. Most will wish that enough of their country remains so that their country can be rebuilt and their way of life continued after hostilities. A nation will wish to preserve its cultural, educational, and religious sites, its reproductive capacity (traditionally represented by women and children), and its non-military economic assets.[9]

Norman's second criticism of Mavrodes is also less than convincing. Norman suggests that rules justified by reference to rule-utilitarian considerations have the tendency to collapse into the (act-) utilitarian principle itself. If, in other words, the greatest utility of the greatest number would be served by breaking the rule, the utilitarian justification of the rule must also justify breaking it.[10] It must be seen, however, that in most cases, following such a rule, and the attendant recognition and strengthening of the rule which serve to ensure that it will be followed in the future, serve human utility better than violating the rule. There are clearly extreme and exceptional cases in which the rule may be trumped simply by virtue of the magnitude of what is at stake, something Norman's own position provides for.[11] This does not, however, refute the argument that these rules serve in most cases as a firm anchor against short-sighted or less-extreme utility considerations. The Second World War is considered—and for good reason—to be the most extreme war to date, where the most was at stake. If world domination by the Nazis—or even just European domination—could have been prevented by bombing German civilians, perhaps such action would have been justified.[12] At the time, however, there was not the slightest evidence that bombing German civilians would have such an effect. First, the assumption that the German people would be so demoralized by the terror bombing that war production would be halted—let alone the idea that the people would revolt against the Nazi regime—is not only psychologically and military-historically unfounded, it is absurd. Even more absurd is the idea that the Nazis, themselves terrorist-minded, would be somehow impressed by the suffering of the populace. More plausible is the idea that the soldiers would be demoralized by the prospect of returning to a bombed-out Germany. The prospect, however, of not returning at all—or, by deserting, of endangering one's family and returning to experience the terror bombing first-hand—was even less attractive; this left only the continued fight, perhaps with the added motivation of hatred towards those who were bombing women and children at home, and an unwillingness to surrender to such an untrustworthy enemy. In short, the terror strategy may have been riddled with pseudo-utilitarian hallucinations, but it was completely free of utilitarian logic—indeed, free from any sort of logic at all. Some American authors justify dropping atom bombs on Hiroshima and Nagasaki with pseudo-utilitarian arguments: the bomb saved the lives, they may say, of a million American soldiers—and Japanese too, it will quickly be added. A single illustration shows the short-sightedness of this argument (to put it mildly): If Truman had refrained from using atom bombs, if he had justified not dropping the bombs on the basis of a respect for the immunity of non-combatants, and had pleaded earnestly for such a principle after the war, if Truman had done all this, it might have made an impression on the American military so deep that it would have retreated rather than carried out a campaign against civilians in Vietnam, and perhaps would never have entered the conflict in the first place. That would have spared the lives of 58,000 American soldiers, of about one million

Vietnamese soldiers and of at least two million Vietnamese civilians. Instead, we are dealing today with a US military (and, apparently, with a majority of American citizens) which would rather kill a hundred civilians than risk the life of a single soldier of their own.[13]

Thus, the principle of the immunity of non-combatants, like the principle of proportionality, does make sense when considered as a convention. This does not mean, of course, that it cannot be justified in some convention-independent way. Michael Green, however, offers an even more radical critique of this than Mavrodes. According to Green, the idea that civilians such as farmers are innocent is simply a relic of the middle ages, the outdated product of an antiquated, hierarchical model of political legitimacy.

Since the chain of authority on this view was from God to government to people, the people had no part to play in legitimising, commanding, or controlling the activities of the government. Thus, their contribution to these were minimal and so was their responsibility for them. One cannot be held responsible for what one cannot and is not obligated to control.[14]

In this political paradigm, the principle of the immunity of non-combatants naturally seems plausible. According to Green, however, this principle is obsolete.

After the French Revolution, war was fundamentally different because political authority and thus responsibility were conceptualised in a fundamentally different manner. In the new paradigm, war became a conflict among nations and peoples involving the total mobilisation of those nations.[15]

Green accuses defenders of the immunity principle—Walzer, Nagel and Holmes, to name a few—of clinging to the medieval paradigm while publicly declaring themselves democrats. Otherwise, they would have drawn the right conclusions.

In a perfect democracy each and every person would be...fully responsible, because if the method of consent has been in operation, each has agreed to the decision reached by that method, or, if not that, to be bound by whatever decision was reached by that method....Within democratic theory, it is not clear that even children, the insane, and the mentally handicapped are innocent. These have guardians who represent their interests. These guardians are still bound by and to the general will of the society in which they find themselves in representing their interests.

Thus, even if as a matter of fact political authorities are responsible for most wars and citizens are usually forced into being soldiers against their will, it is not clear that this absolves them from responsibility if they were responsible for letting themselves be put in circumstances in which they are so passive.[16]

Now, this may be more or less accurate as a characterization of totalitarian democracy à la Rousseau,[17] but the current paradigm is probably the liberal-democratic one. The characteristic of *liberal* democracy is precisely that the individual is *not* required to accept whatever is collectively decided. Rather, such decisions are constrained by the space of individual rights. Green's reference to Locke, of all people, as supporting the idea of the responsibility of the whole populace,[18] including even critics and dissenters, is out of place or, worse, a misrepresentation. Let us examine what Locke himself writes on the topic:

For the People having given to their Governors no Power to do an unjust thing, such as is to make an unjust War (for they never had such a Power in themselves:). They ought not to be charged, as guilty of the Violence and Unjustice that is committed in an Unjust War, any farther, than they actually abet it; no more, than they are to be thought guilty of any Violence or Oppression their Governors should use upon the People themselves, or any part of their Fellow Subjects, they having impowered them no more to the one, than to the other.[19]

Green's criticism is thus rather excessive. A person is not automatically responsible for the crimes of his or her country simply because the country is a democracy. *On the other hand*, it is true that citizens of a democratic state are not as obviously innocent of the crimes of war as were farmers or servants in the Middle Ages. *In this respect*, Green's critique does indeed affect the arguments of Walzer, Holmes and so on. Walzer in particular is quite distinctly concerned with absolving simple soldiers (including those of democratic states) as well as citizens of democracies of as much responsibility as possible—even if they fight in the war or support it enthusiastically.[20] As can be seen from the above quotation, this goes too far for Locke—and rightly so, as the arguments for distancing such individuals from moral guilt are rather thin. Of course, people are routinely indoctrinated, misinformed and manipulated by governments, but in a democracy they *can* discover the relevant information, and in the face of the immense evils presented by war they are indeed *required* to do so before patriotically trumpeting support for, or otherwise taking part in, an unjust war.[21] Walzer, in an outburst of paternal generosity which I cannot quite reconcile with his supposed liberalism, clearly wants to leave the analysis of such information to the "foreign policy elites" (amongst whom, I assume, he counts himself). Coates argues in the same vein:

[T]he individual citizen is rarely in a position to make an informed and responsible judgement about the justice or injustice of the war. The knowledge and expertise required to make a rational judgement of such key criteria as last resort, proportionality and prospects of success are almost always confined to a closed élite even in a democracy. Not only would it be imprudent to allow the public at large to exercise judgement, in this area, but the publication of the sensitive material that informed decision-making would require might jeopardise the security of the state. As a result, whereas in the case of the government the moral presumption must be against war, in the case of the individual citizen the moral presumption may be for war. In either case, of course, that presumption can be (and ought to be) overcome in the face of overwhelming evidence to the contrary.[22]

The last sentence is welcome, but it does not quite suffice. First, many conservatives have argued that individual citizens are also not in a position to judge most other policies, either (such as social security, nuclear power and the European Union). This suggests that a citizen is likewise not in a position to evaluate party platforms, the rationality of campaign promises or the policies of candidates. In other words, if citizens cannot be trusted to decide between war and peace, how can they be trusted to elect representatives or presidents? Coates' argument for a "presumption for war" at the level of individual citizens hardly seems possible without a "presumption against democracy" at the level of the "elites". Luckily, however, Coates' argument is entirely wrong. The "key criteria" of "last resort, proportionality and prospects of success" are hardly quantum physics; they are concepts which ordinary citizens use to make all kinds of decisions on a daily basis, and which they could therefore use also in deciding on war or peace. To do so, of course, they will require the necessary information. In particular, people will need information about specific difficulties and particular aspects which must be kept in mind when applying these concepts to questions of war and peace. Books like Coates' and others provide exactly this sort of information, and bring arguments and approaches to the table for discussion. Such books certainly require a certain level of concentration, persistence and preparedness for discussion (and contradiction) in order to be profitably read. To be understood, they may even require a dictionary, but certainly not a Ph.D. They do not present average citizens with an insurmountable obstacle.

In addition to such theoretical information, individual citizens require information about the actual or potential war. Coates believes that the publication of such information would jeopardize the security of the state. But why? In the case of *ultima ratio* (as also *causa justa*), this is entirely implausible. How could it jeopardize security if it became clear that non-military means could be used to reach the desired goal? (And how could it jeopardize security if it became clear that there was no reason at all to go to war? Wouldn't that indeed improve security?) When discussing the likelihood of success and proportionality, the case may be different. Clearly, if precise details of attack strategies were discussed publicly, the opponent would have the opportunity to prepare for them. On the other hand, it is hard to imagine that the opponent would not have prepared anyway, even without such discussions. He would, naturally, have given thought to the ways in which he could be attacked. Thus, the discussions which occur before a possible war—as opposed to the publication of actual tactics during a war—do not pose a major security risk. Only in exceptional cases would the military develop a brilliant strategy which no one else will have thought of, and which would dramatically increase the chances of success (and perhaps proportionality, too). And because this will happen only in exceptional cases, individual citizens have the right of "presumption against the exception", that is, they may assume that the government's rhetoric about an unbeatable secret plan is nothing more than propagandistic nonsense. In this context, one might wonder what Coates means when he says that it would be "imprudent" to allow the citizenry to make judgements on such matters. Imprudent for whom? Possibly for the governing elite and their friends, who would no longer be able to serve their own private interests—but not imprudent for the populace at large. We rightly have little sympathy when we hear of rock stars who have been cheated by their managers for years without ever realizing it and when they finally do—the manager by this time being long gone—announce "but I trusted him". Similarly with the people who, because the broker "seems so nice and serious", invest money in a stock guaranteed to bring a 300 per cent return, and end up with a 100 per cent loss. Such people are simply stupid, and the same goes for a populace willing to trust the assertions of government on questions of war and peace, rather than insisting on verifiable information, proof, data and documents. For, as Coates concedes elsewhere:

> [N]othing benefits a ruler more than a good war. . . . As a consequence the moral claims made for war need to be viewed with very considerable scepticism.[23]

This insight is hardly reconcilable with a moral presumption for war. Individual citizens have not only a right but also a duty to be sceptical. So, in a democracy, one cannot simply shrug off the responsibility that comes with supporting an unjust war.

So far, we have seen that the distinction between combatants and non-combatants can by no means be reduced to the one between non-innocents and innocents (in the ordinary sense of these expressions).

Robert K. Fullinwider proposes a different approach. According to him, the distinction between combatants and non-combatants cannot be justified with the principle of punishment (which says that only non-innocents may be punished, while innocents must be spared), but with the principle of *self-defence* instead. (Note that, in accordance with legal usage, I use the term "self-defence" here to include cases of defending others.) According to this principle, immediate aggressors would be legitimate targets of violent resistance (and thus in the technical sense of the principle of self-defence "non-innocent"), irrespective of whether one could morally blame them for their aggression. Conversely, individuals who are not immediate aggressors would even then be illegitimate targets if they were morally (co-)responsible for the aggression, for example by supporting, or goading on, the immediate aggressor. Let us have a closer look at Fullinwider's line of argument:

To set the scene, first consider an example. Jones is walking down a street. Smith steps from behind the corner of a nearby building and begins to fire a gun at Jones, with the appearance of deliberate intent to kill Jones.... Jones is afforded no means of escape. Jones, who is carrying a gun himself, shoots at Smith and kills him.

Jones is morally justified in killing Smith by the Principle of Self-Defense. Smith's actions put Jones' life directly and immediately in mortal jeopardy, and Jones' killing Smith was necessary to end that threat. From the point of view of self-defense, these facts about Smith's action are the *only* relevant ones. The moral justification of the killing rests on them alone given the legitimacy of self-defense.[24]

Fullinwider then outlines possible backgrounds for Smith's attack on Jones. For example, Smith's wife may have made approaches to Jones and been rejected by him. In revenge, she told her husband that Jones tried to rape her. Angry and prodded on by the woman, Smith goes looking for Jones in order to kill him. Or perhaps Smith owes gambling debts to the Mafia. They offer to cancel his debts (which he cannot pay) if he kills Jones. Since Smith knows what will happen to him if he does not settle his debts, he agrees. Fullinwider writes:

None of this background information alters the situation from the point of view of self-defense.... Again, suppose that Smith's wife was standing across the street egging Smith on as he fired at Jones. Jones, though he justifiably shot Smith in self-defense, could not justifiably turn his gun on the wife in self-defense. Or suppose the mobsters were parked across the street to observe Smith. After killing Smith, Jones could not turn his gun on them (assuming they were unarmed). No matter how causally implicated the wife or the mobsters were in Smith's assault on Jones, in the situation it was only Smith who was the agent of immediate threat to Jones; the wife and the mobsters were not posing a direct and immediate danger. From the point of view of justifiably killing in self-defense, they are not justifiably liable to be killed by Jones; they are immune.[25]

He applies these considerations to the case of war:

I claim that a nation may justifiably kill in self-defense.... In a war, the armed forces of nation A stand to opponent nation B as Smith stood to Jones. It is against them that B may defend itself by the use of force. The active combatants, their arms, ammunition, war machines and facilities, are the legitimate targets of intentional destruction.

Though A's civilian population may support its war against B and contribute to it in various ways, they stand to B as Smith's wife or the mobsters stood to Jones. For the purpose of justifiably killing in self-defense and from that point of view, the civilian population is morally immune—it is "innocent".[26]

As the principle of self-defence is in any case the most popular for the legitimization of wars, Fullinwider's solution to the problem of the distinction between "innocents" and "non-innocents" in war seems, at first sight, to be particularly elegant and apt. There are, however, certain difficulties. Lawrence A. Alexander remarks:

Fullinwider is correct that *after* killing Smith, Jones may not invoke the Principle of Self-Defense to then turn and kill the mobsters. *The threat to his life has been removed.* ... However, Fullinwider's hypothetical is inapposite when we are discussing whether noncombatants along with combatants may be killed in an on-going war. ... Let us amend Fullinwider's hypothetical to make it relevant to the issue he is addressing. Suppose the situation is the same except that Jones has not yet killed Smith. May Jones invoke the Principle of Self-Defense to kill the mobsters instead of Smith if by doing so he will cause Smith to relent? Of course he may. If the mobsters had a gun trained on Smith and had ordered him to kill Jones, and he were about to comply, Jones not only could, but should, kill the mobsters rather than Smith if killing them would be no riskier than killing Smith and would remove the threat to Jones by removing Smith's motive for killing him.[27]

Alexander concludes that the appeal to the principle of self-defence is therefore not capable of drawing the parting line between legitimate and illegitimate targets of attack in the usual way, the way assumed by the laws of war. For in war, Alexander says, many non-combatants too, whether morally guilty or not, are threats to the defender nation.

A combatant at a camp miles behind the lines is often less a threat than a non-combatant delivering arms and ammunition to combatants at the front.[28]

Alexander's conclusion "that the intentional killing of innocent non-combatants is not necessarily immoral if one accepts the Principle of Self-Defence"[29] can be drawn, however, only when "non-combatant" is defined as narrowly as Fullinwider seems to want it defined. As we saw, only "active combatants, their arms, ammunition, war machines and facilities ... [are] legitimate targets of intentional destruction".

Under the laws of war, however, and on normal interpretations of the theory of just war, supply transports, in particular deliveries of munitions to combat units, are obviously legitimate targets, and those delivering the supplies are combatants. They are, in Murphy's formulation, "engaged in an attempt to destroy you".

On the other hand, one can support Alexander's case with the earlier example of the Nazi farmer. We said above that he is also engaged in "an attempt to destroy you". It seems, then, that we are back where we started. This circle can be avoided, however, if we attempt to shift our perspective away from the fixation on *actual* non-innocence and innocence (interpreted according to either the concept of moral guilt or the principle of self-defence) of potential victims, and instead focus on what the attacker can *know* of the guilt or innocence of potential targets and with *what* degree of certainty he can know it. Let us modify the Jones example to the following Django example. Django stands on the street, his two revolvers holstered, as ten threatening and clearly murderous armed men approach him. Assume that Django has no chance of escape. On the curb stand ten women, two or three of whom are goading the men on. The women falsely and deceitfully present Django to the men as a mass murderer who must be killed. The men actually believe that, if Django is allowed the slightest chance to escape, he will kill again. Django is rightly convinced that the men are acting out of good intentions, and that they have no reason to doubt the horror stories told about him. Giving up is not an option; he knows that he will be lynched (even against the protests of the ten men). Django is also right to assume that the ten men are scared enough that they would disperse if they were not being goaded by the two or three women. He can hear their voices but, due to the distance, cannot tell which women are yelling. The ten men draw their guns. What should Django do? Being a quick-draw sharpshooter, he could kill the ten women as easily as the ten men, and this before any of the men can fire a shot. If he shoots the ten men, he will have shot ten people who are, from a moral standpoint, innocent. From the standpoint of the principle of self-defence, all ten are, however, legitimate targets. If he shoots the ten women, he will shoot two or three people who are, according to both moral and self-defence principles, non-innocent; on the other hand, and more difficult still, the other seven or eight are entirely innocent. Even if the numbers of innocent and guilty are switched among the women, the answer is intuitively clear: Django may shoot the men, but not the women.

How would this look if only the two or three women doing the inciting stood on the curb? I agree with Alexander that Django would be allowed to kill them in self-defence *if* he knew that killing them would remove the direct danger to himself. In what realistic situation could Django know that, though? In any real situation, killing the women would make it even more likely that the men would shoot him.

The application to war is clear. An infantryman or helicopter pilot can surely recognize enemy soldiers, tanks and munitions transports more easily than he can the disposition or financial transactions of a farmer. He can recognize the soldiers by their weapons and their behaviour, which demonstrate that they are engaged in an attempt to kill him or damage his country. Not so in the case of the farmer and not, by the way, in the case of enemy radio or television propagandists, either. Even if the latter were to broadcast continuously the words "let us bathe in the blood of our enemies", it is entirely unclear that destroying the radio tower or killing the journalists would lessen the danger. Enemy soldiers obey commands, react to threats and would be inundated with propaganda even without radio or television, which is targeted, rather, at the civilian population. To attempt to justify attacks on radio stations and journalists by reference to the principle of self-defence is under nearly all circumstances a laughable, indeed shameful, misuse of that principle. Such attacks are indeed intended as punishment, or as simple attempts to clear the airwaves for the attackers' own propaganda. He who punishes with death a public expression of opinion—or a call to arms of enemy soldiers, or even contrary views—himself deserves punishment. It is even worse when one considers that it is much harder to justify the killing of innocents (e.g. janitorial staff) as a side effect of an act of punishment in war than it is to justify it as a side effect of an act of collective self-defence. In the latter case, under some circumstances one could say that the deaths of the innocents was acceptable as part of an attempt to save a larger number of innocents, that is, as the lesser of two evils. In the former case—killing as a side effect of an act of punishment—that would be true only if the principle of self-defence (or the principle, to be discussed below, of a justifying emergency) is *also* already applicable anyway. Only when the actions of enemy journalists do indeed result in deaths can the potential deterrent effect of the punishment of such journalists prevent further deaths from journalistic propaganda in the present or future conflicts. As already said, however, the assumption that this condition is met is unfounded. And putting the punishment of the guilty before the protection of the innocent is, while being a moral precept from the Old Testament—and thus commended in some lands—morally perverse. It is not for nothing that the laws of war treat attacks upon radio stations (which are not used for military purposes) as a war crime. For the same reasons this also goes for attacks on most other civilian resources.

If we interpret Fullinwider's approach in terms of self-defence not ontologically (concerning the question as to what is the case) but rather epistemologically (concerning the question as to what one can know or justifiably assume), it indeed delivers—in contradistinction to Anscombe's approach centred on moral guilt—a convention-independent justification of the distinction between combatants and non-combatants which is in agreement with the laws of war. This only holds true, however, if the analogy between individual and national self-defence which Fullinwider relies on can bear the weight which is placed upon it. But here serious reservations can be raised. They concern the question whether killing in war can be justified by the analogy *at all*. In other words, and in exact opposition to Green's criticism, the distinction between combatants and non-combatants is abolished here not by declaring everyone a legitimate target, but by declaring everyone an *illegitimate* target. Norman puts a first problem as follows:

The first thing to be said is that it is, as it stands, *only* an analogy. As such, I do not think it can do the work of justification. The right of individual self-defence, if it justifies anything at all, justifies the killing of the attacker to defend the life of the victim. In attempting to justify a war of self-defence, what we have to justify is, again, *literal* killing, the taking of hundreds, thousands or even millions of human lives. According to the self-defence analogy, however, what are being defended are not literally lives, but their collective analogues, the life (and liberty) of the community.[30]

If, so Norman continues, the defence of an individual's right to life justifies overriding another individual's right, namely the aggressor's right to life, then, taking the analogy seriously, a state's defence of its right to sovereignty and territorial integrity would also have to justify overriding an aggressor state's right to sovereignty and territorial integrity.

That, however, is not, of course, what we were supposed to be arguing for. We needed a justification for *killing* to defend the community. The analogy, understood strictly as an analogy, cannot provide one.[31]

At this point one might say that one does not need the analogy because in war one has to do with *literal* self-defence, too: The aggressor-soldier shoots at the defender-soldier, who shoots back. The aggressor-bomber bombs the fellow citizens of the defender-soldier, the latter shoots down the former. Against this reasoning, however, three objections can be raised.

First, perhaps we are dealing in such cases with an act of legitimate self-defence, and hence with a legitimate killing, only if the fatal attack of the aggressor could not have been averted by other reasonable means. Assume, for example, that Django, embittered and disinhibited after the experience described above, is asked by a man—to whom he has no financial duties—for a dollar for a whiskey. Django refuses and goes away. As a result, the man threatens him from behind with a revolver and demands the dollar again. Django says: "Django won't pay today", swirls around, draws, shoots and kills the man. Killing a man only because one wants to save a dollar, however, is excessive. Django should have forked out the dollar.[32] Analogously, the shooting and bombing of the aggressor-soldiers can perhaps be avoided from the start if one gives them what they want. Is it really necessary to shoot at these soldiers only because they want to take away a certain oil well from you, or maybe even just a small isle of sheep which is uninhabited anyway? Some authors argue, of course, that against such encroachments one surely must have the right to *some* form of resistance, for example to non-violent resistance. If this non-violent resistance then provokes a violent reaction of the attacker and to that extent creates a self-defence situation, one is once more justified in defending oneself. In other words, since one is justified in creating the conditions for one's own self-defence, one can just as well shoot right away.³³ This argument, however, can also be reversed: If it is clear that the initially non-violent resistance will in the end lead to the killing of a person because of a dollar, shouldn't one then completely forgo resistance? This is doubtlessly a good question, but the answer is, it seems to me, not as clear as both sides think. Let us modify our last Django example again. Here Django is not threatened from behind. Rather, he has the correct and justified conviction that the whiskey friend will immediately draw his gun and shoot without further commentary if Django refuses to deliver the dollar, so that he, Django, would have faced with this development no other option for saving his life than to shoot his opponent in self-defence. It appears to me, now, that Django *should* fork out the dollar, but that he nevertheless has the *right* not to do so.³⁴ Justice does not have to give way to injustice. On the other hand, one does not always have to insist on one's rights. To do so anyway can, in certain situations, not only be pedantic but also reprehensible. With a view to Kant's terminology we can distinguish here between rights-based duties (*Rechtspflichten*) and virtue-based duties (*Tugendpflichten*). By keeping the dollar and hence bringing on the fatal fighting situation for his adversary, Django by no means violates his adversary's rights; consequently he does not violate his own rights-based duties, either. However, he does violate, as we may say, a general commandment of humanity, the commandment of solidarity with one's fellow humans. While one may be forced to abide by one's rights-based duties and be punished for infringements, one's violations of virtue-based duties may only be answered with reproof, indignation, rejection and the like. Therefore, if Django shoots instead of paying, he may deserve to be insulted for acting like a "brute", but he does not deserve to be considered and treated as a murderer or manslaughterer.

The first pacifist objection, thus, only works, if it does at all, in those cases in which the object defended by the defender is out of proportion to the killing of the aggressor. In order to make the objection into a general argument against killing in war, one would have to show that, contrary to first appearances, practically nothing justifies, let alone makes irreprehensible, the killing of an aggressor as a consequence of one's bringing about a self-defence situation by resisting a rights violation. David Carrol Cochran argues in this direction:

Since existence is the most basic feature of human beings (that which provides for all else), its protection is our most basic moral claim.... So the only thing that can justify taking a human life is life itself. This is the case of life versus life, and it is the only case where overriding the prohibition against killing another human being is permissible.[35]

Surprisingly, Cochran does not even consider the possibility that the right not to be mutilated, raped, enslaved or in some other form drastically violated in one's freedom could justify killing an aggressor. This makes his position appear quite dogmatic right from the start. But above all, it is simply wrong. On the one hand, there are things which are worse than death. Life is not only the basis of joy, but also of pain. On the other hand, his first premise rightfully suggests that existence is so fundamental *because* it provides for everything further. But this means, in turn, that an existence is only good to the extent that it indeed provides for these further things. Why, then, should an existing being only be allowed to kill in defence of its existence, but not also in defence of a certain fundamental value of its existence? Incidentally, Cochran explains that "even a case of life versus life is not enough ... to justify such an override". Rather, the attacker's *guilt* of facing the attacked person with the alternative of dying or killing turns the scale in favour of the life of the attacked person.[36] But since, according to Cochran, the life of the attacker is initially as valuable as the life of the one attacked, one requires only the slightest pinch of guilt in order to reach the said imbalance. Someone who tries to kill an innocent, though, is not only the slightest bit guilty, he rather burdens himself with a very considerable guilt. But the same also holds true for someone who tries to mutilate, rape, enslave or in some other way drastically harm an innocent. Thus, even if in such cases an attacked person cannot throw the whole weight of his life, but only the allegedly lesser weight of his integrity and freedom into the scales, why shouldn't this be compensated by the great guilt of the aggressor in such a way that the attacked person gains the right to, if need be, lethal self-defence in these cases, too? Cochran does not answer this question; nor do other pacifists.

Frank de Roose, however, is of the opinion that armed resistance is not worthwhile for the defenders, except when they are defending themselves in a war of extermination. Thus, he does not argue, in contradistinction to Cochran, that the attackers' lives are too valuable, or that the attackers are not guilty enough to be killed, but that, in a way, the defenders cannot, with good reason, be sufficiently desperate to kill in self-defence.

[P]resumably, people prefer death to a life characterized by unbearable suffering, but do not prefer death to a life characterized by bearable suffering.... As long as situations offer the possibility for some kind of resistance, the suffering that they produce will not be unbearable. The reason is that the possibility for resistance is tied up with the presence of hope for a better future, and that, as long as there is such hope, suffering can be endured.... Such situations do, therefore, not provide a moral justification for self-defensive killing.[37]

De Roose makes it sound here as if the defenders faced the following alternative: life in non-violent resistance or death in armed struggle. However, the alternative to non-violent resistance (which, by the way, can be lethal too) is not death in armed struggle but merely the *risk* of death in armed struggle; and while human beings may indeed prefer a bearable suffering to death, they by no means necessarily prefer it to the mere risk of death. Rather, what is decisive here is the question as to what the degree of suffering, the risk of death and the chances of liberation by non-violent resistance as well as those by armed resistance, respectively, are. In fact, it is not difficult to see that many human beings, for example the members of several resistance movements, prefer the death risks and liberation chances attached to violent struggle to the perhaps higher survival but lower liberation chances in the case of non-violent resistance. De Roose's pacifist argument is a non-starter.

Let us come to the second objection against the legitimization of killing in war by the appeal to literal self- or other-defence, respectively. This objection claims that soldiers, even those on the side of the aggressor, are *innocent* and that one cannot bring the right to self-defence to bear against innocents. I have already rejected such general presumptions of innocence above. For the sake of argument, however, we shall presume for a moment that the aggressors really are innocent, for example because of some permanent indoctrination to which they were inescapably exposed. Does this mean that one may not kill them if this is the only chance to save one's own life from their attack?

Judith Jarvis Thomson disputes this emphatically. Among other things, she adduces the example of a truck driver who is drugged through no fault of his own and tries to run over a certain other human being—let us stick to Django (this is not Thomson's choice of names). Django's only chance to prevent this is to blow up the truck. He does exactly this with the bazooka he happens to be carrying with him. This is the case of the innocent aggressor, and Thomson regards killing the truck driver in order to save the attacked person as clearly legitimate. In fact, she goes even further with another example. Django sits on his deck when a man who is on the cliffs above him falls. If the man lands on Django, Django will be killed, but the man will be saved by the cushioning of the impact. (If both died, numerical considerations become relevant, which we want to exclude here.) Django's only chance not to be crushed by the man is to vaporize him with a ray gun he has at hand, and he does exactly that. The falling man is no aggressor—he does not attack, after all—but merely, on account of his falling, a threat. ("Threat" is used here throughout as a *terminus technicus* that includes *persons* and *things* posing a threat.) In this case, too, the self-defence is, according to Thomson, justified.[38] I agree with her. The justification of self-defence seems to me to be in both cases intuitively completely convincing.

The principle which she bases the justification of both cases on, however, is less plausible; and of course especially authors with diverging intuitions point to this fact—and the intuitions of different authors in this field diverge considerably. (This notwithstanding, I believe that Thomson's—and my—intuitions with regard to these two examples correspond to common sense). According to Thomson, the killing of the innocent aggressor, as well as the killing in the case of the innocent threat, is permitted because of the alleged fact "that they [i.e. the attackers] will otherwise violate your right that they not kill you, and therefore lack rights that you not kill them".[39] Against this it has been rightfully objected that it is quite strange to say, in the case of the falling man, that he violates the rights of the person upon whom he falls (and whom, hence, he kills). Would we say of an avalanche which has killed someone or of a tile which has fallen from a roof and fatally injured a passing pedestrian: "They have violated his right to life"? Obviously we do not use such language. The reason for this is that avalanches and tiles are not capable of being subjects of intentional action.[40] A person's right always corresponds to the duty of others to respect it. Obviously, avalanches and tiles cannot reasonably be declared to be the bearers of duties. Therefore, one cannot have rights with respect to them which they could violate. The falling man, of course, has duties. But he has them as an actor, as a subject, not as a mere object of unfortunate circumstances. He has the duty not to throw himself onto an innocent in order to kill him; but he does not have the duty not to be the innocent victim of an accident in the course of which he falls on another innocent and thereby kills him. Such a duty would not make any sense; one cannot be obliged to things which are beyond one's control: "Ought" implies "can".

If Django is permitted to kill the falling man, he may do so not because this man violates Django's rights, but because he, in turn, does not have the right to kill Django. But he would kill him as the avalanche and the tile, too, kill those upon whom they fall.[41] On the other hand, everyone has the right to attack an aggressor or a person who represents a threat, as I have already emphasized above.[42] Of course, the above argument which states that the right to attack an aggressor protects the other individual rights seems to be hardly applicable in the case of innocents who present a threat (and perhaps not even in the case of innocent aggressors). From the right to kill an aggressor, no (or at best a very weak) deterring effect emanates in such cases. In the present case, however, we do not need this effect, anyway. It should be noted here that the right to attack an aggressor has been discussed above in the context of the doctrine of double effect. The social function of the deterrent effect of the right to attack an aggressor was adduced there as an explanation for why this right can, under certain circumstances, legitimize accepting the death of third parties as a side effect of such attacks. At the moment, however, we are not talking about the killing of third parties but about the killing of (innocent) aggressors and those who represent a threat themselves. The reason why such a killing seems to most to be intuitively and rightfully justified is probably that we do not regard it as *reasonable* to expect a person rather to let himself get killed than to kill an aggressor or avoid a threat (be the aggressor or threatener both ever so innocent). To behave like this is, as philo- sophical terminology has it, *supererogatory*, that is, it goes in an angelic way (so to speak) beyond the fulfilment of one's duties. But why is such an action unreasonable? The strong human drive for self-preservation does not present a sufficient justification. For then it would also be justified if someone who needs a heart transplant secretly killed the patient in the next room who has a donor pass, foreseeing that he will then receive his heart. Self-*defence* is a narrower concept than self-preservation—and therefore, inciden- tally, the attempt to argue against the justification of the killing of innocent aggressors or threateners, with the claim that such actions would then have to be permitted too,[43] is of no avail. An obvious justification for the unreasonableness is the *immediacy* we are usually dealing with in self-defence situations. If someone shoots at you or tries to run you over and flatten you with his truck, or if someone is about to kill you with his falling body, the danger is not an indirect one but, well, immediate. In other words, one is *under pressure* and with one's back against the wall. Michael Otsuka, however, objects against this: Being under pressure may indeed be an *excuse*, but it is by no means a justification.[44] If the cliff in the example of the falling man is so incredibly high, or if because of some disturbances of gravity the man's fall is at the beginning so slow (but nonetheless fatal) that Django is not at all under pressure (which shall change nothing about the inescapability of the self-defence situation), but able to meditate and to read poems before deliberately and calmly vaporizing the falling man with his ray gun, then there would not even be an excuse for this course of action, let alone, allegedly, a justification. In my view, however, killing in self-defence is intuitively clearly justified in this case, too. And this intuition can be supported by argument. For the distinction between the self-defence situation and the self-preservation situation (e.g. of the organ transplant example) is by no means dependant upon the criterion of immediacy. The falling man has, as already stated, no right to kill Django, but is about to do so. The patient with the healthy heart, of course, also has no right to kill his fellow patient—but he is, anyway, not about to do so. He only lies there non-aggressively and unthreateningly. On the other hand, he obviously has the right to keep his heart. From this follows the duty of the other person not to interfere with his execution of this right, for example by killing him in order to get his heart. Since the falling man, for his part, has *no* right to kill Django, Django has *no* duty not to interfere with his attempt to do so. Of course, the pacifist will argue that the question is precisely whether one may interfere by *killing* him. However, the burden of proof seems to reverse here to the disadvantage of the pacifist. Why shouldn't Django kill the falling man? De Roose urges us to bear in mind:

[I]f there is no moral difference between one person rather than another getting killed, and if at least either of two persons will get killed, one is under no obligation to kill the one rather than the other person, if one happens to be either of these two persons. The fact that neither of the two persons is morally responsible for the situation they are in, makes it a tragic situation, but that in itself need not affect the moral permissibility of self-defensive killing.[45]

The pacifist, no doubt, will again fall back here on his cherished distinction between killing and letting die. However, I have already adduced an example above which shows the implausibility of this distinction.[46] Moreover, this implausibility is also and especially demonstrated by the present example. For there is a further, absolutely decisive distinction between self-defence and self-preservation. With reference to the latter, it is intuitively out of the question that the cardiac patient sacrifices himself for the healthy one if he does not kill him. He does not die *in order that* the other live. This would only be the case in the reverse situation, namely if the patient with the healthy heart says: "Kill me and give my heart to the other patient." Yet, it would *also* be the case if Django abstains from using the ray gun and has himself crushed by the falling man, who would thereby, *ex hypothesi*, be saved. *Sacrificing oneself for another person, however, is the paradigmatic case of a supererogatory action*—it is heroic, it is holy, but it is certainly not everyone's "damn duty". And for this reason it is indeed *unreasonable* to expect Django to abstain from self-defence on behalf of another man's survival.

Incidentally, Otsuka, who has already been mentioned, adduces an example which is somewhat uncanny even to himself and in which the distinction between acting and abstaining from action seems not to play a role:

Imagine that you are holding a flagpole upright out of patriotism for your country. You come to realise that if and only if you do nothing but continue to hold this flagpole, a falling [Innocent] Threat will be impaled on the pole, but you will be unharmed. If you drop the flagpole, then the [Innocent] Threat will land on you, killing you but surviving the fall herself.... I am prepared to swallow, as a consequence of my argument, the claim that you may not continue to hold the flagpole.[47]

Otsuka overlooks in his subsequent discussion, though, that it is not the fact that, in order to save the falling person, one has to do something here (put down the flagpole) instead of merely abstaining from doing something (not firing the ray gun) *in itself* which rouses such strong intuitions against the immunity of innocent threats in this case, but rather that due to this fact the sacrificial character of the rescue of the other person at the cost of one's own life is particularly emphasized. Nevertheless, in both cases, in the example of the ray gun as well as in the one of the flagpole, such a rescue has this sacrificial character. I agree, therefore, with Otsuka that the two cases are not distinct in morally relevant regards. But from this follows the consequence which is exactly opposed to his intention—killing is not prohibited in both cases, but allowed in both cases. Otsuka may well be prepared to swallow the heavy chunk he has served himself; others will—with good reason, as I hope to have shown—not muster such willingness.

Thus, the second objection, too, against the legitimization of killing in war by an appeal to literal self- or other-defence, has been rejected, even under the concession that soldiers are innocent.

It is worthwhile, however, to explicate some interesting implications of the preceding line of argument. Although I have spoken of the right to attack an aggressor or a threat, I have not claimed that Django has a right to attack the innocent threatener. Rather, I said that he may attack him. One does not have a *right*, though, to everything one *may* do. It is necessary to say a few words here on the logic of rights. Rights (or most rights, in any case), as has already been said several times, are not absolute. For instance, we speak of the right to life, but this right does not go so far as to comprise the immunity of an aggressor from being killed by someone practising their right of self-defence. We speak of the right to the free expression of one's opinion, but we accept limits to this right, too. The same holds true for the right of the free development of one's personality and so on. The scope of a person's rights are sometimes restricted by similar rights belonging to other persons, sometimes by other rights of other persons. A person's right to free speech can be limited by another person's right to the protection of his dignity, for example against insults. A point that is rarely clearly seen is that not everything which is legitimized through rights is thereby also legitimized *as* a right. Assume a hunter is granted the right to shoot any stag he likes in a certain forest. Simultaneously, a zoo director is granted the right to catch any stag he likes for his zoo. (We might just as well assume two hunters with similar hunting rights.) From these rights it follows that one may stop neither of the two from shooting or catching a stag in this forest. It does not follow at all, however, that both have the right to shoot or catch a certain stag S which they both confront, noticing their competitor, at the same time. For unlike some forest hiker who lacks competing rights, each may stop the other from catching or shooting the stag, namely by anticipating the other. But this does not involve a right to anticipate the other. For if the hunter had a right to anticipate the zoo director, the latter would not be permitted to anticipate the former. But he is permitted to do so. We thus have a case here where the following is true: The conflict of two general rights of equal weight leads, in a certain case, to the consequence that these rights mutually restrict one another, thereby producing, in case of conflict, more special permissions. The two rights to kill or catch, respectively, any stag in the forest legitimize killing or catching the stag S, yet they do not legitimize these options of acting *qua* rights, but merely *qua* permissions.

The right to attack an aggressor or a threatener is, furthermore, not absolute. This right has its greatest force in the case of non-innocent aggressors or threats. In that case it also goes far beyond self-defence, even if we disregard the punishment of aggressors. The reason for this lies, of course, with the *guilt* of the aggressors. This guilt also entails that in cases in which one cannot save oneself in some other way from the aggressor's attack or its negative consequences (if the attack is already over), one has a *right* to divert the threat (e.g. death)—which would otherwise befall oneself—to the aggressor who is its cause. Phillip Montague states the following conditions for this:

(i) individuals $X_1 \ldots X_n$ are situated so that harm will unavoidably befall some but not all of them; (ii) that they are so situated is the fault of some but not all members of the group; (iii) the nature of the harm is independent of the individuals who are harmed; (iv) Y, who is not necessarily included in $X_1 \ldots X_n$ is in a position to determine who will be harmed.[48]

The attack on the aggressor, thus, is not legitimized here by a *present* aggression but by his culpably causing the harm. This cause can lie in the past. Montague adduces the example of a doctor who wishes for the death of a cardiac patient and therefore swallows the pacemaker the patient needs. The only chance to get the pacemaker quickly enough to save the patient's life is a hasty operation on the doctor, which would, however, be fatal to him. Hence, one faces here a situation in which either the innocent patient or the malicious man has to die. If, however, one of the two has to die anyway, and one has to decide who it is going to be, then one clearly should, says Montague, decide against the person who has culpably brought about this situation. I agree with him. (Whether such a procedure is legally licit is another question; we are dealing here with the moral question.)

The guilt of the aggressor has in particular the consequence that he relinquishes the right to defend himself against (proportionate) violent countermeasures. Thomas Hobbes, though, thinks that one may expect no one not to fight for his own life if it is threatened, not even if he has provoked this threat through his own illegitimate attack.[49] Yet, something which can at best serve as an excuse is again confused here with a justification. That it cannot be a justification can be seen by the fact that, on this condition, the following act is not murder: Smith, who is an excellent shot, shoots at Jones, narrowly missing Jones' head, in order to provoke Jones' counter-attack. Jones, being confronted with an attack on his life, draws his gun and wants to shoot back. Smith anticipates him "in self-defence": the second bullet hits Jones exactly between the eyes. To claim that this is no murder is, of course, utter nonsense. This problem is recognized by some defenders of Hobbes' thesis. The solution which proponents of Hobbes' thesis offer lies in declaring the "self-defence" of the aggressor legitimate, while declaring, on the other hand, that the bringing about of the self-defence situation is illegitimate. On the grounds of this illegitimacy, the "self-defending" aggressor would then, presumably, still be a murderer.[50] I say "presumably", because it is mysterious how somebody who kills another person *justifiably* can be the murderer of that person.[51] Actually, the aggressor could merely be held responsible here for "illicitly bringing about a self-defence situation with lethal consequences". However, we do not happen to see it that way. Rather, we do consider him a murderer. In other words, we assume that he did *not* have the right, or even so much as a justification, to shoot back at the defender attacked by him. If need be, as soon as the other drew, he would have had to drop his gun and surrender. If this would have clearly resulted in his own death (e.g. because the defender could not react quickly enough to the change of the situation), this would not justify the killing of the defender, but only underline that the attacker should have refrained from the attack in the first place if he did not want to commit a murder by this killing.

The situation is completely different with an *innocent* aggressor or an innocent threat. In the case of the non-innocent aggressor, his guilt—that is, his violation of the rights of others—brings it about that his own rights are curtailed to such an extent as to allow the defender to proportionately attack him without violating his rights. If he can only be stopped by killing him, this simply means that his right to life must give way to the other's right to self-defence. But since the innocent threat or the innocent aggressor does not violate the other's right to life, as we maintained against Thomson, *his right to life remains intact.* This is also true, on the other hand, for the innocent attacked or threatened person. Thus Django has a right to life, and so does the falling man. Here the brief excursion into the logic of rights comes to bear. In this case, the two aforementioned rights collide in the same way as did the rights of the hunter and the zoo director. This is to say, at the point of their collision they cannot be upheld any more as rights (because they are not compatible with each other); rather, they give way to permissions (which are compatible with each other).[52] In short, *not only may Django vaporize the falling man, but the falling man may also kill him in order to prevent that.* This conclusion has a very significant application to the case of war. We have seen above that Anscombe's approach, whether she realizes it or not, deviates from that regulation in the laws of war according to which the killing of just combatants (i.e. of combatants who wage a justified war with licit means) by the opposing side is justified. However, this is at first also true of Fullinwider's approach in terms of self-defence (a point which is raised neither by him nor by Alexander). For an aggressor has, as we have seen, by no means the right violently to defend himself against a proportionate counter-attack which has been provoked by his attack when the attack was initiated with the intention to kill. Yet the analysis of the right to self-defence which we have just carried out possibly offers a solution here.

To be sure, though, we have only for the sake of argument assumed that the soldiers of the aggressor side, too, are innocent. In most cases they are not. Even Cochran at least admits:

[W]hile many soldiers may not be guilty of the war itself, they are not completely innocent within the course of that war either, because they intentionally take up weapons and use them to kill.

But he continues:

Is this form of culpability enough to justify killing them? It is not.... All soldiers are aggressors, in that they seek out and try to kill enemy soldiers, but, at the same time, all soldiers act in self-defence, in that they try to kill enemy soldiers before those soldiers can kill them.... This kind of equal culpability cannot provide the "critical asymmetry" required to justify self-defensive killing.[53]

However, we saw in the example of Django and the falling man that this asymmetry is by no means necessary. One could be inclined to conclude now that things cannot be different in the case of two *equally non-innocent* participants, either. To the extent that there is no morally relevant distinction between the two, none of them, it seems, can be obliged rather to die himself than to kill the other. But while the falling man, insofar as his fall is not an action at all, does not violate Django's rights, and Django does not violate the falling man's rights because he has no other means to defend his equivalent right to life against the other's, this is different in the case of two hostile soldiers who act in ways which are equally culpable. For they may both evade the situation without a violation of higher ranking or equivalent obligations (otherwise they would not behave culpably). Thus, there is indeed no justification for killing in self-defence here. Each soldier would be obliged to refrain from killing the other.

Yet, consider the following example. In a little town in the Wild West in which the prohibition of guns is enforced, Smith and Jones have been threatening one another with death for several days. They hate each other, and both of them know that. However, neither of the two would premeditatedly and intentionally kill the other. But this is something they do not know about each other; in fact, they have good reason to believe the exact opposite, given their permanent virulent speeches and their respective dubious pasts. In the evening they both leave the town without the other's knowledge—with their guns. Still later in the evening, Smith sees a campfire in a small forest. He approaches it, hoping to be invited to a cup of coffee. When he is only 10 metres from the fire, the man who is sitting there looks up— and it is Jones, of course. In panic both reach for their revolvers and open fire at each other.

In my view, we are dealing here with a situation in which neither of the two has done something which would make his own right to life yield to the other's right to attack an aggressor. This is indeed a situation in which both are aggressors as well as defenders—or perhaps neither of them are either of the two, but both are equally fighters. Since each one of the two retains his right to life in full (and no utilitarian reasons override it), neither of them can shoot the other *justifiably*. Both *should* have abstained from drawing their guns and firing. This abstention would have corresponded to the commandments of morality. By not abstaining, they failed to act rightfully. For this, however, they cannot be blamed. (Analogously, penal law distinguishes between an objective breach of law, on the one hand, and full-blown guilt, on the other hand.) Thus they both act excusably.

It seems, of course, that excluding the justification already suffices for Cochran, but I doubt that a pacifist really can be content with it. Killing in war would then be illegitimate all right, but not reprehensible, let alone, as pacifists claim, extremely reprehensible.

The reply would probably be that indeed the soldiers do not act extremely reprehensibly, but that the politicians and generals who send them into the fray do. But isn't this reply intended also to convince the population and the potential soldiers to oppose war? Can this be achieved with the assertion: "But if there will be a war, anyway—it will not be our fault; and if you shoot other people there—that will not be your fault, either." I doubt it.

Besides, one must observe that, although soldiers are not always or nearly always innocent, they sometimes can be innocent. This is not, as the example of the ten men threatening Django shows, prevented by merely taking up arms, for at issue here is not "non-innocence" in terms of self-defence, but in terms of morality.

But can there not be more than only mutual innocence, namely mutual justification? Well, one could imagine the following example. After having killed the ten men in legitimate self-defence, Django is on the run, hunted by a posse. Finally, he is brought to bay by one of the pursuers. This pursuer justifiably (though incorrectly) believes that Django is guilty and wants to arrest him. The pursuer aims the rifle at him and demands that he unbuckle his guns. Django knows, however, that even in a fair trial he would be sentenced to death, since the circumstantial evidence and the testimonies tell against him; in addition, he knows that, once without guns, he will no longer have a chance to escape (the pursuer could never be persuaded). Django runs for his horse. The rather slow pursuer shouts: "Stop or I will shoot." Django dives headlong to the side, draws and fires. His adversary responds. We are dealing with a situation here in which the pursuer could actually have spared himself the self-defence situation. However, against this stands his duty as a law enforcer. Hence, he not only does not enter the self-defence situation culpably, *but he is even obliged* to risk the self-defence situation. On the other hand, Django too is not acting culpably. The self-defence situation was forced upon him, and he was clearly justified to flee instead of delivering himself up to certain death. The situation between Django and the pursuer is thus morally equivalent to the one between Django and the falling man. From this follows that *both* are justified to shoot at each other.

It is important here to emphasize that this equal justification does not result from the mere fact of the *innocence* of the two.

This becomes clearer if we look at an essential difference between the example of Django and the falling man on the one hand and the example of Django and the ten men on the other. For the falling man is, as we have said, no actor at all, at least not with respect to his falling. His eventual shooting is an act, but his falling is not. Therefore, as we have also said, he cannot violate Django's rights with this falling. He could do this with his shooting at most; but since the threat that originally emanates from him (the falling) simply does not constitute a violation of Django's rights, his own rights do not give way to those of Django. This, in turn, entails that the shots he reacts with at Django's vaporization attempts are no rights violations either, but are indeed permitted. The original attack of the ten men on Django, however, *is* an act, namely an act which violates Django's right to life (because they *erroneously* regarded him as an aggressor), or rather an act that would violate it if successful. Therefore, the ten men are *excused* for their attack in so far as they could not avoid the error, but they are not justified in attacking. Django's pursuer, of course, also acts, but his act is not only excused, but also covered by the law enforcer's right to bring a putative murderer to justice. In any case, I see no special reason to assume that this right does not have the same rank as the right to life and the right to self-defence. Hence, both Django as well as his pursuer can justifiably shoot at each other.

It might seem, however, that in war there can hardly be cases like this one. For both sides cannot wage a just war (while they can both wage an unjust one).[54] They can both *believe* that they are in the right, but they cannot both *be* in the right. Therefore two armies cannot be in the same relation to each other as Django and his pursuer, but only as Django and the ten men. This would mean that the usual view, according to which in war the soldiers of *both* sides have the *same* right to kill the soldiers of the other side, is *wrong*. Jeff McMahan in particular has emphatically argued against this usual view, which he calls the "orthodox view"; McMahan himself defends the "moral view". However, he thinks that in the framework of the latter, one can, perhaps, grant at least innocent unjust attackers the justification for self-defence against the counter-attack of the attacked.

[A] case can perhaps be made for the claim that Innocent Attackers, while merely excused for their initial attack, are nevertheless justified in engaging in self-defense against the defensive counterattack by the victims of their initial attack.[55]

But not even that seems to be correct. I have adduced the example above of Smith who, in order to provoke Jones' defence, initially shoots narrowly past his head and subsequently, when Jones' defence indeed occurs, fires the deadly shot. Let us slightly modify the example. Smith is the bodyguard of a politician and sees how Jones, whom he incorrectly but reasonably considers to be a professional killer, points a gun at the politician. (What he does not know is that the politician has just asked him for the gun because he wants to take a look at it. Jones only gives it to him.) Smith shoots at Jones, misses him, Jones aims his gun at Smith in order to shoot him, but Smith anticipates him with a second shot and kills Jones.

Why should Smith be justified in this killing? With his attack he has violated Jones' rights, after all. This rights violation makes Smith's own right to life—insofar as Jones, as we of course again assume, can save his life only by killing Smith—yield to Jones' right to attack an aggressor. Therefore, he cannot be justified in shooting at Jones. On the other hand, Jones has not only a *justification* (in the sense of mere permission) for self-defence, but also a *right* to it. This means, however, that others are obliged not to prevent him from exercising this right. But Smith tries to do precisely that with his second shot. Thus, he violates a right not only with the first but also with the second shot. It is hence not by chance that, I believe, we would expect a third person, for example the local sheriff, who can save one of them by shooting the other and who knows about Smith's confusions with respect to Jones, to save Jones and not Smith. If he decided otherwise, we would demand a *justification*. For *Smith* has committed a *mistake*, not Jones—and this is morally quite relevant. If two parties are equally innocent, this does not yet mean that there can be no morally relevant distinction between the two. A person can also bear responsibility for things of which he is not guilty. This is not only a legal rule, it is also morally plausible. If Franz innocently lost the book Fritz has borrowed from him, who has to compensate for the damage? Clearly the one, of course, who has, and be it only innocently, made the mistake, namely Franz. The same holds also for our case. As Michael Otsuka states:

[A] morally responsible agent may be held accountable for engaging in such activity that puts the life of a potentially innocent person at risk even if she acts from the justifiable (but false) belief that this person is a villain. When one is in possession of rational control over such a dangerous activity as the shooting of a gun at somebody, it is not unfair that if the person one endangers happens to be innocent, one is by virtue of engaging in such dangerous activity stripped of one's moral immunity from being killed.[56]

But is Jones also not responsible for a potentially lethal attack, namely for his counter-attack on Smith? Yes, but he is thereby attacking someone who is *responsible for an illegitimate attack*, he is attacking him in defence against this original attack; Smith, on the other hand, attacks in his defence someone who is *not responsible for an illegitimate attack*. This is obviously a decisive difference.

The orthodox view, then, appears to be wrong. The soldiers of the two hostile parties are not equally justified in killing each other. This "moral view" is, nevertheless, still at least partially compatible with the laws of war. For they, as a conventional legal system, do not maintain that both parties are *morally allowed* to kill one another. Instead, they declare that soldiers may not be *punished* for killing enemy soldiers (e.g. in a prisoner-of-war (POW) camp during the war, or by a tribunal after the war). That soldiers may kill one another without punishment, however, is also conceded by the moral view with respect to some cases—namely those in which both sides are *excused* (whereby one side may even be in the right). On the other hand, the moral view can be reconciled with the laws of war only up to a point. Whereas the laws of war excuse soldiers for fighting in the war so long as they behave according to the principles of *jus in bello* (i.e. so long as they do not slaughter civilians or torture prisoners), the moral view does not: it requires soldiers also to adhere to the principles of *jus ad bellum*. Soldiers are moral agents, and as such bear responsibility for their actions and decisions. They cannot transfer this responsibility to the authorities. On an issue as important as whether or not to fight in a war, one has, as described above, a duty to make an informed and considered decision. Soldiers who fight on the unjust side and could have known and prevented it without great danger to themselves (e.g. by draft dodging, deserting or intentionally missing when shooting at the enemy) are morally guilty, even without killing civilians. For the *soldiers* on the just side, it seems, are also innocent (so long as they adhere to *jus in bello*).[57] If the soldiers on the unjust side kill these innocent soldiers, *they are committing criminally negligent homicide, at least*. If these soldiers *know* that their side is in the wrong, *by killing enemy soldiers they commit manslaughter or murder.*[58]

However, there is a problem with McMahan's argument that significantly reduces its scope. For if, as McMahan claims,[59] only people responsible for unjust threats can be liable to attack, innocent bystanders are not liable to attack. Therefore, by killing them one would *wrong* them. One might still be, all things considered, *justified* in wronging them, but one would not be *just* in doing so. Now, in modern wars combatants regularly kill innocent bystanders—which is called "collateral damage". Therefore, combatants, including those on the "just" or justified side, are *morally responsible for an unjust threat* and hence *liable to defensive attack,* this time by the soldiers of the other, "unjust" side who might try to protect their innocent bystanders by destroying the unjust threat posed by the enemy. Moreover, there is no reason why such defensive attacks against just combatants should not be proportionate.

A way to escape this conclusion would be to argue that one wrongs innocent bystanders only by *intentionally* attacking them, while killing them as a side effect of one's use of force against a legitimate target would not wrong them, would not be unjust.[60] However, this argument presupposes the correctness of the doctrine of double effect or of some more or less equivalent principle. But, as we have seen, this doctrine is mistaken.

A second way to escape the above conclusion would be to argue that the combatants on the unjust side could avert or ward off the unjust threat posed by the combatants on the just side by retreating. If they would just stop warring against the just side, the unjust threat posed by the just side would disappear. This may be true if the entire country were to stop warring, but single soldiers, as McMahan recognizes in a slightly different context, or even regiments and other units, are hardly in a position to "effect the coordinated surrender of their entire country and certainly could not do so in time to forestall the wrongful [or, in our case, unjust] action".[61] Thus, the most promising way for the soldiers on the unjust side to stop unjust attacks on their innocent bystanders by the just side would be to keep to their posts and fight back, for in most circumstances they cannot reasonably expect to overcome the collective action problem and induce sufficient numbers of their comrades to give up fighting.

A third way to escape the above conclusion is to change the premises and claim, as indeed McMahan does: "[J]ustification defeats liability: one is liable to defensive killing by virtue of responsibility for an unjust threat only if one acts without justification. This seems intuitively plausible; for it is hard to see how one's moral immunity to being killed could be compromised merely by one's acting in a way that is morally justified."[62] But such a move seems to be *ad hoc*. In particular, *wronging* someone *by posing an unjust threat to him* is hardly something one "merely" does, not even if one does it justifiably.

Besides, even if one tries to explain away the liability of the justified (but unjust) attacker in this way, it still does not follow that justified soldiers cannot be justifiably killed because of the unjust (but justified) threat they are posing. This can be seen by means of one of McMahan's own examples:

A tactical bomber fighting in a just war has been ordered to bomb a military facility located on the border of the enemy country. He knows that if he bombs the factory, the explosion will kill innocent civilians living just across the border in a neutral country. But this would be a side effect of his action and would be proportionate to the contribution that the destruction of the facility would make to the achievement of the just cause. As he approaches, the civilians learn of his mission. They cannot flee in time but they have access to an anti-aircraft gun.[63]

And he later explains:

Because the tactical bomber's justified action would wrong the civilians, they are permitted a proportionate defense. And killing him would be proportionate. But because he is not morally liable to be killed by them, they will wrong him if they kill him in self-defense. He too, therefore, . . . is justified in killing them in preemptive self-defense.

He adds:

This reasoning is also compatible with the plausible view that third parties are not, other things being equal, permitted to intervene.[64]

First, this view is not plausible at all. Assume the innocent civilians are children. Would their parents not be permitted to intervene on their behalf? Obviously, they would. At the very least, it is quite counter-intuitive to deny them this permission. And why should third parties not be allowed to intervene in such a situation on behalf of their spouses, lovers, friends and, most importantly in this context, compatriots? After all, traditionally one of the main advantages (and obligations) of shared citizenship has been cooperative protection against external threats. This is such a situation.

Second, contrary to what McMahan seems to suggest, the situation does not change in a (for our purposes) morally relevant way if the innocent civilians do not live across the border. Innocent civilians are no less innocent when they are citizens of the country engaged in an unjust war. Thus, they are not liable to be attacked and killed (be it collaterally or not). If they are, they are *wronged.*

I conclude that McMahan has not established that the combatants on the unjust side cannot justifiably kill combatants on the just side. They can do so in cases in which the justified combatants pose an unjust threat. They do so in most modern wars. In the Second World War, for example, Allied soldiers posed a threat to innocent people on the German side. German soldiers, therefore, could justifiably kill "just" soldiers. There are, however, cases in which McMahan's argument applies, namely when the combatants of the just side (perhaps a weak invaded country) do not pose any unjust threat, typically because they lack the means (or the will) to attack the enemy in its own country (and therefore do not pose a threat to the innocent on the enemy side) and do not threaten their own innocents. These cases have long been rare, although the more or less neocolonial wars fought by the United States and some of its allies in Nicaragua, Grenada and arguably Afghanistan and Iraq seem to somewhat shift the balance. Thus, historically the relevance of McMahan' argument is much more restricted than he thinks. In current political circumstances, however, its relevance is growing.

Let us finally turn to the third objection against the approach in terms of self-defence. It says that in war, self-defence necessarily plays only a minor part, and is therefore not suited for a justification of war. It is already contained in Cochran's following statement, which has been cited above:

All soldiers are aggressors, in that they seek out and try to kill enemy soldiers.

He elucidates it in more detail as follows:

[W]arfare ... fails to meet the requirements that one may kill in self-defense only as a last resort and that one may do so only at the time one is actually under attack. In war, soldiers do not try to avoid killing the enemy (doing so could bring a court martial). They actively look for the chance to kill opposing soldiers as a first resort, not as a final one. Furthermore, as Eric Reitan points out, soldiers in war do not wait until they are under immediate attack to fight. To be successful in war, soldiers must attack preemptively, but this requires attacking enemy troops at times when they are not acting as aggressors.[65]

Cochran calls himself a war pacifist. In contradistinction to an absolute pacifist he is not against all violence, in fact, not even against all lethal violence. Rather, he accepts the legitimacy of the right to self-defence.[66] But he does not consider it sufficient for a justification of war. We have already seen two reasons and rejected them as insufficient. *This third objection, however, is absolutely correct.* Not, as we have seen, in the sense that there can be no justified self-defence in war, but very much in the sense that a large part of the killing of soldiers in war has nothing to do with justified self-defence (not even on the just or justified side), and that this is a necessary feature of war. An army which in war attacks hostile units only when it has already been attacked by them would—barring unlikely and exceptional circumstances—indeed have few prospects of success. Does (war) pacifism thus have the last word?

Not quite. In the whole debate on the question as to the extent to which war can be legitimated, it is for the most part overlooked (inexplicably) that there is a far more promising starting point for such a legitimization than the right to self-defence, namely the concept of a *justifying emergency.* That an emergency can justify extreme measures is widely accepted, not least in German penal law, in which §34 reads:

Whosoever, in order to avert a not otherwise avoidable present danger to life, body, freedom, honour, property, or another legally protected interest, acts so as to avert the danger to himself or others, does not act illegally if, upon consideration of the conflicting interests, namely of the threatened legally protected interests and of the degree of the threatened danger, the protected interest substantially outweighs the infringed interest. This, however, is true only if the act is an adequate[67] means to avert the danger.

The decisive difference between self-defence and a justifying emergency is that the latter requires for its applicability only a *danger* which is present and not otherwise avoidable, but not a present *attack*.

Suppose a man camps with his family somewhere in the Canadian wilderness. Over the radio he learns that a plane transporting prisoners has crashed nearby. The prisoners are five mass murderers; they have survived, equipped themselves with the guns of their dead guards, and have already killed several other camper families. Now they are heading in his direction. The attempt to flee with his children would be hopeless; as he knows, the murderers are good trackers and march with superior speed. To be caught by them in unprotected terrain would mean death. However, it is very likely that the murderers will pass on their way through a rocky, narrow pass. There the only possibility for survival is to lay a deadly ambush for them. If he allowed only one of them to escape, this would also result in the death of his family. Thus, the father of the family goes with his rifle to meet them, seeks out a suitable cover at the upper edge of the pass and, when the five murderers indeed appear, shoots them dead.

Different people have different intuitions. I for my part regard the conduct of the man not only as justified, but even as required in light of his duties towards his family. The transfer of the emergency situation, and hence of the justification of deadly resistance that accrues from it to the case of war, obviously does not present a problem.

A war pacifist may of course be tempted to apply the first two objections against the approach in terms of self-defence also against the one in terms of justifying emergency; but these objections evidently fail against the latter for the same reasons, discussed above at length, that they failed against the former. First, killing in an emergency situation can obviously be proportionate in war, too; and second, the innocence of two hostile opponents would change nothing about their emergency rights. If, after their clash, Django and his pursuer have found cover in a grove after narrowly avoiding the shots of the other, and each of them knows that only the one who employs the tactic of surprise and shoots the other dead without notice can survive an inevitable further clash, then both are justified in trying to do precisely that. The same would hold good for soldiers who oppose each other innocently. To be sure, I have just explicitly stated that soldiers cannot face each other in such a constellation of mutual innocence (in the emphatic sense of not being responsible for their aggression or threat) in war. But this helps the pacifist all the less, as we have already seen. The fact that neither party can be innocent does not exclude that one of them is innocent after all. If, now, there is a party to a conflict whose survival or freedom is illegitimately and in such a way endangered by approaching troops that it can avert this danger only by itself attacking the approaching troops, then it is very well justified in doing so.

In addition, the exercise of the emergency right against an illegitimate threat that cannot be averted in any other way is, as the example of the man and his family has shown, not only permitted for saving oneself, but also for saving others. Therefore, friendly units can protect each other from hostile units by attacking them in time. The typical strategic and tactical conduct of war between hostile military formations can thus be justified.

What about the distinction between non-innocents and innocents, or between legitimate and illegitimate (human) targets? In the approach which invokes the terms of a justifying emergency it largely corresponds, with respect to the unjust side, to the one between combatants and non-combatants. But only largely. Sometimes a grave present danger for life, body or freedom cannot be averted from oneself or another in any other way than by an attack on civilians or non-combatants. If they are to be held *culpable* for the danger, an attack on them with the purpose of averting the danger is morally justified, as we saw above.[68] But if they are innocent, one faces in the "consideration of the conflicting interests, namely of the threatened legally protected interests and of the degree of the threatened danger" grave moral dilemmas. These dilemmas will be the focus of our attention when we approach the topic of terrorism.

In this chapter we have discussed four approaches to distinguishing the "non-innocent" from the "innocent", that is, the legitimate from the illegitimate human targets of attack: the *moral guilt theory,* the *convention theory,* the *self-defence theory* and the *justifying emergency theory.* Of these, the convention theory uses the utilitarian principle solely to *de*-legitimize certain acts in war—namely attacks on non-combatants (in Murphy's sense). The other three approaches can be used to legitimize single acts in war, but only the justifying emergency theory is able to justify the entire war. But couldn't the moral guilt theory do this, too? Only if one considers the principle of double effect as a component of the approach. (For it is, as Holmes rightly says, impossible to wage modern wars without killing innocents.) However, the proportionality principle of this theory has rather little to do with *moral guilt,* but is instead based on a consideration of moral costs and utilities. In other words, such a "moral guilt theory" speaks of guilt when it already really has emergencies in mind. In order to do justice to the facts while maintaining clear analytic borders, then, only a theory which allows attacks on the (sufficiently) guilty while condemning attacks on the innocent can be considered a proper guilt theoretic approach.

Each of these approaches has its own morally valid principle at heart: the principle of moral guilt, the rule-utilitarian principle, the principle of self-defence and the principle of justifying emergency. The important right to attack an aggressor also plays a role, of course, in so far as the right conceded by the guilt principle (i.e. to use violence against a guilty person if necessary) and the right conceded by the self-defence principle (i.e. to violently defend oneself against an aggressor) are two sides of the right to attack an aggressor. The various approaches differ from the principles they are based upon, however, in that each approach raises its respective principle to an absolute status, and uses it as the one and only measure for distinguishing between legitimate and illegitimate targets and acts. One correspondingly arrives at new approaches when one applies more than one principle. As we have seen, Anscombe's approach makes use of both the moral guilt principle and the principle of justifying emergencies—even if it claims not to. Fullinwider too, however sceptically, does allow for the possibility of connecting his favoured principle of self-defence with the moral guilt principle.[69] As stated above, all four principles are valid, and they interact with one another. For example, one of the morally protected interests which must be considered in the weighing process required by the principle of justifying emergency is that the innocent be free from punishment, and this, of course, leads to the principle of moral guilt, which serves to protect the innocent. Moreover, these principles can conflict, as did the guilt principle and the self-defence principle in the case of the innocent aggressor. Such conflicts arise at the level of severity and situation-relative priority, but not at the level of validity.[70] Both principles are valid standards for morally correct action. In other words, in the event of such conflicts the "suppressed" principle gives way to the other, but only within certain bounds: up to this point, but no further! The continued validity of the guilt or innocence principle, even in the case of the innocent aggressor, can be seen in the fact that the application of force is allowed *only to the extent* that it is necessary to avert the danger (whereas in the case of a guilty aggressor the aggression may perhaps be "paid back with interest", that is, punished). The principle of self-defence, indeed, recognizes these limits explicitly, in that it does not allow for anything beyond what is necessary for defence. On the other hand, there is no such explicit recognition of the principle of self-defence within the moral guilt principle. This is normally the case in conflicts between principles. In view of such conflicts, as also is the case with interactions between principles, a process of *weighing* is required, one which is undertaken with sufficient judgement, circumspection and sensitivity to the particulars of the situation. The morally correct action cannot be derived from the principles in the way the value of an unknown variable can be derived from a system of equations; it cannot be deduced as a conclusion from premises. Rather, it must be found on a case-by-case basis, in light of the particulars of the situation. This is not a matter of applying principles which are already determinate in rank and scope for each case; rather, the judgement must be made by interpreting the principles and the situation in such a way that the interpretation of the principles and the characterization of the situation influence each other. The morally relevant aspects of the situation are identified in light of the principles, and the principles are weighed in light of the morally relevant aspects of the situation.

In order, then, to evaluate the meaning and implication of these principles, and thus also the results of our analysis, it is important to keep the following consideration in mind: that the principles interact with one another, and that the particular interactions depend on the concrete situation. From this perspective, the rejection of the orthodox view set out above in favour of the moral view that soldiers on the unjust side, even if they adhere to the principles of *jus in bello*, are still incurring moral guilt when they kill opposing soldiers who do not pose unjust threats is less radical in its practical implications than it might seem to be at first glance. For not only do soldiers on the justified side, as I have pointed out, still pose unjust (and culpable) threats in many if not most cases and are therefore liable to attack, but there are also strong *rule-utilitarian* grounds which limit the moral guilt principle significantly. As McMahan observes:

[T]here are no impartial institutions competent to determine which soldiers do deserve punishment and how severe a punishment they deserve.... Even if the victor in a war is the side that fought in a just cause, it could not possibly administer punishment to large numbers of soldiers in an informed and impartial manner. And matters are of course much worse if it is the unjust side that emerges victorious.... If the practice were sanctioned, [the victors] would doubtless be moved to seek vengeance, under the guise of punishment, against soldiers who had justifiably resisted their wrongful aggression. Finally, the expectation that ordinary soldiers would face punishment at the hand of their adversaries in the aftermath of war would deter either side form surrendering, thereby prolonging wars well beyond the point at which fighting might otherwise cease.

The laws of war, therefore, have to diverge from the morality of war.[71]

This last sentence, however, postulates an unpleasant divergence that is unnecessary in our model. On the basis of the rule-utilitarian principle, itself a valid moral principle, adhering to the laws of war is *morally required*—though only up to a point, of course, as shown above.[72] The usefulness of the laws of war consists not only in their protection of soldiers from unjust punishment, but also in their protection of non-combatants—and indeed the very foundations necessary for the continued existence of the nation—from soldiers.[73] If, however, (as one may argue) soldiers or fighters on one side do not keep their end of the bargain and violate the convention, the other side does not have to, either. Yet this attempt to justify attacks on civilians is still undermined by the principle of moral guilt, because the civilians—in so far as they really are innocent—cannot do anything about the crimes of their soldiers. The *soldiers*, however, can. They have broken not only the silent agreement with the soldiers of the opposing side, but also their agreement with the *civilians* of the opposing side. It follows that these civilians are no longer required to stay out of the fray. Moreover, on the principle of self-defence, they may defend themselves and their property, family and friends. But won't they, by taking up arms, become combatants and thus legitimate targets, even if they strictly limit their defence to the attackers, refraining from inflicting collateral damage? Well, in the sense provided by the laws of war, yes, but certainly not morally. For none of these fighters on the just side, from a moral perspective, is a legitimate target—this is the insight of the moral standpoint. Decisive, however, is the fact that the enemy soldiers can neither legitimately nor innocently attack civilians under arms (people, we may imagine, shooting at the enemy from their own homes). Their attack on the basic living needs of a population is itself an obvious violation of *jus in bello*, and makes the soldiers *morally guilty* (unless, of course, they are forced at gunpoint to attack), while the civilians remain innocent, since in such a case the moral principles allow the violation of the normal laws of war. (It is not even clear that this would be a violation of the laws of war. The important point here is that even if it were, it would be morally allowable in this situation.) The rule-utilitarian principle does not forbid people in such a situation to take up arms, and the moral guilt principle, as well as possibly even the self-defence and justifying emergency principles, give people a *right* to break the convention. This right *forbids* the soldiers from preventing the civilians from exercising it. If the soldiers do not obey this, they not only contravene moral rules, but also make themselves culpable—they are simple murderers. The only way of not continuing to commit murder would be to retreat.[74]

In this context, let us examine the following example. Various extended families, at home in some archaic land, simply know that disputes between them will always erupt into armed conflict, but they nevertheless wish to keep the damage arising from such conflicts within certain limits. In order to achieve this, the families agree that only men may be attacked and that women and children may not attack anyone. One day, the men of family A attack family B, including the women and children. Because a majority of the men have already been eliminated, some women and children pick up weapons and defend themselves. The men of family A respond to this by saying: "You're breaking our convention, and are attacking us. Now we can kill you in self-defence." This appeal to self-defence is just as illegitimate as the case in which Smith, who first fires a shot that misses Jones, uses Jones' counter-attack as an excuse to kill him "in self-defence". Of course, it is possible that many A-men attacked only B-men in the original attack. These A-men would be, in my view, perfectly entitled to fight the women and children in self-defence—but only insofar as they are not responsible for creating the situation where they must defend themselves. An A-man, being shot at by women and children because his two comrades next to him opened fire on them, can after all move the women and children to cease fire—namely, by killing his comrades in self-defence, that is, in defence of the women and children against precisely these comrades. The A-men who knew that others would fire upon women and children, but who went along anyway, are also responsible for creating the situation. They have no right to self-defence, unless, of course, they have come along to hinder their comrades. When they see, however, that they have failed to persuade their comrades to desist, and that they can stop them only with violence, they must do so or—the morally inferior alternative—run away. Otherwise they lose their right to self-defence.

This can also be illustrated in the Israeli occupation of the Palestinian territories. Let us take the massacre in Jenin in April 2002. Of course, the UNO has since declared that no massacre occurred in Jenin. That is, by the way, a rather astounding finding, when one considers that Israel refused to allow an inspection commission into the land (why not?), and that the following report appeared in the Israeli media:

After the first moments of the fighting, when a commander was killed . . . the instructions were clear: shoot every window, spray every house—whether someone shoots from there or not. . . . The point is that they were inside the houses. The last days, the majority of those who came out of the houses were old people, women and children, who were there the whole time and absorbed our fire. These people were not given any chance to leave the camp, and we are talking about many people.[75]

Or the following report of a brave bulldozer driver (his unit was later commended):

For three days, I just destroyed and destroyed. . . . They were warned by loudspeaker to get out of the house before I come, but I gave no one a chance. . . . I didn't give a damn about the Palestinians, but I didn't just ruin with no reason. It was all under orders. . . . I am sure people died inside these houses, but it was difficult to see. . . . I found joy with every house that came down, because I knew they didn't mind dying, but they cared for their homes. If you knocked down a house, you buried 40 or 50 people for generations.[76]

If, by the word "massacre", one understands the indiscriminate slaughter of civilians, this was obviously a massacre.[77] The last remark of this bulldozer driver and mass murderer shows quite clearly that the basic living needs of the population, the entire nation and its future were attacked. The convention of immunity for non-combatants (including immunity of civilian property) is thus being spurned in this case. Tanya Reinhart (an Israeli Jew, one may note) has described the Israeli policy towards Palestinians as drawn-out ethnic cleansing. Drawn-out, because more spectacular mass murders (which have also happened, for instance, in Sabra and Shatila)—acts like mass executions or deploying chemical weapons—damage Israel's image in the world and hence its interests (or at least the interests of the military). Instead, one uses other means. Because death tolls arouse great media attention while the number of the wounded is less widely reported, strategies like targeted mutilation are used.

More than seven thousand Palestinians were reported injured in the first five weeks of the [second intifada], many in the head, legs, or knees by carefully aimed shots, and, increasingly, live ammunition. Many will not recover, or will be disabled for life.[78]

These mutilations are, as reported by a delegation of the *Physicians for Human Rights*, often used in non-life-threatening situations.[79] Shooting Palestinians in the eye with rubber bullets is also a part of this strategy. Similarly, Israel does its utmost to destroy the infrastructure of the Palestinian society, including important institutions, computers and files, as well as by destroying olive trees en masse, and by undermining the health and food supplies of the population.[80] This is really a war against an entire people, fought out of simple greed for land. It is, therefore (and many Israeli Jews agree, though it would not change anything if this were not so), entirely appropriate to speak of a campaign of ethnic cleansing. There is no excuse for such a campaign. The "War on Terror" is surely none at all. A war on terror should surely be aimed at terror, rather than at spreading terror on an even greater scale. The Israeli soldiers involved in such ethnic cleansing, even if only through simple membership in the organization carrying out these policies, are murderers, maimers and manslaughterers, or at least the helpers of such. The Israeli army and the administration of the Israeli state are criminal organizations. Because of this, it would be absurd to deny immunity to a Palestinian who shoots from his house at the machinery of destruction aimed at him—that is, a Palestinian who is acting in self-defence against a present, not just illegal but also immoral, attack on his life, liberty and property. This is also so when such a person acts not in self-defence, but rather under the conditions of a justifying emergency, for instance by trying to stop the enemy before they reach the settlement. Insofar as the enemy is morally guilty, it has not only no licence, but also no excuse for returning fire. And insofar as *they*, the enemy, are responsible for breaking the convention (Montague's selection rule plays a role here), they have themselves freed the other side from any requirement to adhere to the convention. Thus the other side does not become guilty by not following the convention. Neither legitimate nor excusable targets (aside from *proven* terrorists) are available to the Israeli aggressors. For the Palestinian defenders, however, whether combatants or civilians, the current conditions of occupation make Israeli soldiers (with the likely exception of those who refuse to serve beyond the green line) legitimate targets under the justifying emergency and moral guilt principles. The occupiers are legitimate targets at any time, and would remain so even if attacks on them were not necessary to bring an end to the occupation, for the guilt of the occupiers allows the defenders to punish them in this way. (Insofar as there are no overwhelming utilitarian reasons, such as a catastrophic counter-reaction, not to punish. The already catastrophic situation of the Palestinians can, however, hardly be much worsened by Israel without also negatively affecting Israel.)

We thus see that, contrary to widespread opinion, not only must *jus in bello* be taken into account in *jus ad bellum*, but that *jus ad bellum* must also be taken into account in *jus in bello*. One must strictly avoid placing the aggressor and the defender on the same level and considering the first party's breaks of conventions as neither more nor less bad than those of the second. This is not a call for double standards; on the contrary, it follows directly from the application of the same moral standard. The *same moral* norms and principles are valid for both sides but, insofar as the two sides *do not* behave in the same way and *are not* in the same situation, it follows that in certain situations they are subject to different moral imperatives and bound by *conventions* to different degrees (though they are bound by moral principles to the same degree).

I have argued over the last pages in particular that the principles presented and analysed in this chapter would, in some situations, interact in such a way as to trump the convention requiring that civilians wishing to maintain their immunity may not take up arms. An even trickier question, however, is whether there may be situations in which the situation is reversed: in which the immunity of non-combatants is trumped, so that direct attacks on civilians are allowed. This question is none other than the one as to whether terrorists can be justified in certain circumstances.

5

The Ethics of Terrorism

Can terrorism be justified? We have understood terrorism here, roughly, as the direct attack on innocents. And it is this, contrary to Coates' and Thompson's opinion, that makes terrorism *prima facie* reprehensible, and not the alleged lack of an allegedly necessary "legitimate authority" in the sense of a legitimate representative.[1] Nevertheless, we cannot leave the question of definition at that, for "terrorism" is mostly used as a polemical concept, too. The word has an extremely bad ring to it and many negative connotations. A direct attack on innocents may consequently be described more leniently or more sternly, depending upon whether one calls it an "act of war" or "terrorism". Indeed, terrorism seems to be for many the very instantiation of evil, even worse than all crimes of war. At best "genocide" seems to carry similarly satanic or apocalyptic connotations as "terrorism". This, of course, contributes to the fact that "terrorism" is preferably used for the acts of the *others*, not for one's own actions. In fact, there is hardly a concept on earth which is used by the usual suspects with such an unsavoury and reprehensible moral double standard as precisely this one.[2] This double standard and propagandistic usage is therefore to be met with an adequate and clear definition—one that avoids saying: "If two perform the same deed, it is not necessarily the same."

Unfortunately, the larger part of the Western press and of Western politicians have, out of docility, malevolence, ignorance or stupidity, made precisely this motto their own. This can be seen by the consistent implicit application of the definition of terrorism provided by the US State Department, according to which only subnational or underground organizations can commit terrorist acts in the first place.³ The Nazi regime would not have been, according to this definition, a regime of terror. But such a conclusion hardly corresponds to our linguistic and moral intuitions. Therefore we must reject as inadequate such a definition of terrorism, which opens the door for the double standards of states—and this may very well be precisely its purpose. Incidentally, we have some allies in this endeavour in our other US friends, namely the FBI and the US Department of Defense. For according to them terrorism is

the unlawful use of force or violence against persons or property to intimidate or coerce a Government, the civilian population, or a segment thereof,
in furtherance of political or social objectives,

or, respectively,

the unlawful use of—or threatened use of—force or violence against individuals or property to coerce or intimidate governments or societies, often to
achieve political, religious, or ideological objectives.⁴

Whether an act is one of terrorism or not is a question to be decided by the act itself, and not with reference to the perpetrator. Bruce Hoffman, however, whose view is representative of that of others as well, thinks that such a position plays

into the hands of terrorists and their apologists who would argue that there
is no difference between the "low-tech" terrorist pipe-bomb placed in the
rubbish bin at a crowded market...and the "high-tech" precision-guided
ordnance dropped by air force fighter-bombers from a height of 20,000 feet
or more that achieves the same wanton and indiscriminate effect on the
crowded market-place far below.⁵

But in fact, whoever does not apply a double standard plays only into the hands of objectivity and universalism, whereas Hoffman himself plays into the hands of partisanship and state terrorism. This partisan attitude is manifest in his distorting comparisons. Thus he explains that, although armies too have attacked civilians, oftentimes legal steps were taken in order that the delinquents might be made responsible for their actions.

By comparison, one of the fundamental *raisons d'être* of international
terrorism is a refusal to be bound by such rules of warfare and codes of
conduct.⁶

First, we also notice such a refusal in the handling of the Taliban prisoners by the United States, as well as in the extreme hostility on the part of this state towards the International Criminal Court. Second, Hoffman is comparing apples and oranges when he seeks to compare legal possibilities with the disposition of perpetrators. If we avoid this skewed view, we will have no difficulty in recognizing that not just crimes of war, but also subnational acts of terror are pursued legally (the latter even more frequently). We will also see clearly that there are instances *both* of armies *and* of subnational groups which accept certain rules in the waging of war and the application of force. (In fact, Hoffman himself stresses the fact that ethno-nationalistic and separatist groups and, in particular, left-winged terrorists are also subject to certain ethical constraints in their choice of targets.[7])

Hence it remains the case that terrorism is to be defined as a method. C. A. J. (Tony) Coady offers an already classical definition. Under "terrorist act" he understands the following:

A political act, ordinarily committed by an organized group, which involves the intentional killing or other severe harming of non-combatants or the threat of the same or intentional severe damage to the property of non-combatants or the threat of the same.[8]

(Coady's further remarks suggest that he does not mean just any political acts, but rather acts of *violence*.) This definition did not escape criticism, even outside of objections in the style of Hoffman. Thus, Virginia Held warns that, according to Coady's definition, the 1983 bombing of US Marine barracks in Lebanon in which 241 people died, most of them US soldiers, would not be an act of terrorism. But this, according to Held, would be arbitrary.[9] In fact, it is only consistent. If US attacks on military targets in which primarily soldiers are killed are celebrated in the media as "surgical operations", we cannot suddenly speak of terrorism when the situation is simply reversed. Held also deems it "peculiar" "to make a very sharp distinction between the September 11 attack on the World Trade Center, which was certainly terrorism, and the attack that same day and with entirely similar means, on the US Pentagon building, which on this definition would not be".[10] I fail to detect any peculiarity here. To give an analogy: why should it be "peculiar" to make a sharp distinction between, let's say, the shelling of an undefended Russian hospital by the German army on a certain day in September 1943, which would certainly have been a war crime, and the attack that same day with entirely similar means on a Russian infantry division, which would not have been a war crime? Sharp distinctions are not so much peculiar as strongly needed. Incidentally, to claim, as is sometimes done—and that certainly *is* peculiar—that the US soldiers in the barracks were not really combatants because, well, they were just in the barracks, is quite simply nonsense. The soldiers were not in Lebanon as tourists on vacation, but *as soldiers*, they were *deployed* in a country where a *civil war* was going on. Of course they were combatants (at least in any traditional understanding of this notion). Similarly, the military headquarters of a superpower that "defends its interests" with armed force all over the world, if need be, is not a civilian installation but—at least according to the laws of war—a legitimate target for all those who defend *their* interests against this superpower with armed force, if need be.

There is a further line of criticism against Coady's definition. Held thinks that terrorism is political violence that at least "usually spreads fear beyond those attacked".[11] Some other authors, however, go farther and claim that the spreading of fear or the intent to spread fear is not only a usual but a *defining* characteristic of terrorism. This would be a further argument against Coady's definition. Jeremy Waldron distinguishes between "Jack-Benny-style coercion" and "Arendtian terrorization". The former "leaves room and is intended to leave room for rational calculation on the part of the victim" while the latter "overwhelms rational deliberation".[12] For the latter, he adduces the example of a bullion robbery "where the robbers poured gasoline over a security guard and threatened to set him alight if he did not open the vault". He claims that the guard can hardly be expected to engage in rational calculation under these conditions. Instead, his mental processes might run along the following lines:

My God, I am soaked in petrol: he is going to kill me. Shall I give him the combination—He has got a light. He is going to set fire to me. Is it worth ... —He is going to set fire to me. He is going to set fire to me! I am going to burn![13]

And he reckons that something like this could also be done to a whole population, or at least to significant parts of it. He realizes, however, that it "is one thing to do all this with the U.S. Air Force; it is another thing to do it with the puny resources and mostly inconsiderable weapons that those we call terrorists have at their disposal". Yet, he claims that "there may be a level of abstraction at which the terrorization we discussed in Section 4 [the Arendtian terrorization] reveals something in common with the impact that ordinary terrorists can reasonably expect to have".[14] He explains:

Terrorism is not just simple coercion. It looks to the possibility of creating a certain psychosocial condition, ψ, in a population that is radically at odds with the range of psycho-social states $\{\phi_1, \phi_2 \ldots, \phi_n\}$ that the government wants or needs or can tolerate in its subject population. The terrorist group performs various actions—explosions, killing, etc.—which tend to put the population or large sections of it into condition ψ. The terrorist group does this with the aim of giving the government a taste of what it would be like to have its subject population in condition ψ. And it threatens to continue such actions, with similar effects, until the government yields to its demands.
In this account ψ, might be a state of terror . . . [or] something short of the kind of "bestial desperate panic" that Arendt described but nevertheless a state or condition that governments cannot afford to let their populations fall into or languish in for long.[15]

However, it is not clear how a little girl could, by slapping someone in the face, give him a taste of how it would be to be knocked out by the heavyweight boxer Vladimir Klitschko. Waldron does not explain, but simply assumes here, that terrorists commit deeds that "tend to put the population or large sections of it into condition ψ". And if ψ means a state of Arendtian terror or something very close to it, this is simply and obviously wrong.

Yet Waldron thinks that the "short-term collapse in economic activity" and the fall of the Dow Jones index after the attack of September 11 or the "collapse of the tourist trade in Israel . . . in the wake of recent suicide bombings" can support his case. "These economic effects may be attributable to widespread fear that outrages of the sort that have already occurred are likely to continue—that is, they are symptoms of general insecurity."[16] This may well be the case, but fear and "general insecurity" are hardly terror or anything close to it. In fact, not all values within the Dow Jones dropped. Some were not touched at all. The values that dropped most were those of insurance companies and airlines. That, however, does not seem to be so much the expression of a lost capacity on the part of investors for rational deliberation as an exercise of it. Likewise, to assimilate the "loss of a cheerful bullish mentality among consumers and investors"[17] to something analogous to Arendtian terror pretty much ignores the difference from the Jack-Benny-style coercion that Waldron at first stressed so much. The cheerful bullish mentality among consumers and investors will also disappear with the end of an economic boom (or with a long winter), but that does not mean that consumers and investors are terrorized or have lost their capacity for rational calculation.

Waldron then goes on to speculate about what it would be like "if the U.S. were to experience explosions in [public places] at the rate of (say) one or two a month, each causing the sort of casualties that recent suicide bombings have caused in Israel", and he says that we "need not surmise that this would result literally in *terror...* in order to see that even the taking of reasonable precautions by large numbers of people in the wake of such experience would radically alter the way that life is lived in this country".[18] Now we are suddenly talking about *reasonable* precautions. Such reasonableness, however, seems incompatible not only with *literal* terror but also with anything coming close to it. In fact, it seems more and more that the "certain psycho-social condition" Waldron is talking about could refer to just about everything "that governments cannot afford to let their populations fall into". It could, for example, refer to the psycho-social condition of wanting to have another government; or to a growing understanding of the motives of the terrorists, an understanding that is pretty much at odds with the one of the government; or to a growing awareness of certain situations the government cannot afford the population to be aware of; or to opposition towards the government's foreign policy. Why should terrorists not aim at some of *these* things? In fact, seeing that the Allies were not able to instil Arendtian terror in the German population in the Second World War even though they "dehoused" practically all major German cities, terrorists will hardly expect to achieve better results with their "puny" resources. Nevertheless, even if they therefore—as is safe to assume—do not act with a view of instilling Arendtian terror in the target population, we normally still consider them as terrorists if they blow up civilians in skyscrapers. Thus, the idea of terror being necessarily a part of what terrorists aim at is misleading.[19]

Onora O'Neill has a different approach. Terror does not necessarily aim at instilling *terror*, she claims that terrorist "speech acts" aim at fear.

But they do not do so explicitly. The speech acts of terrorists have a distinctive, disconcerting and self-effacing character. A threat is conveyed, yet is deliberately veiled. Those who are threatened are left to decipher to *whom* the message is directed, *whether* the message is serious or hoax, *how* dangerous the threat is, *whether* the threatened action can be averted.[20]

However, she admits herself that terrorists can make very clear demands and threats, and adduces the case of the hostage-taking of a theatre audience in Moscow in the autumn of 2002. Yet, if this was a terrorist act, then terrorist acts (or the "speech acts" that convey threats and demands) do *not* have to be veiled or self-effacing. Moreover, the Moscow hostage-taking is hardly the only example. She considers the IRA a terrorist organization, but the threats of the IRA are actually quite easy to "decipher". O'Neill's analysis simply does not correspond to the reality of terrorism. It is also very unrealistic when she claims that terrorist organizations have to use those "veiled" communications because otherwise they would give too much away about themselves and thus make their capture easier. Given the existence of videotapes which can be easily dropped off at a television station or sent, and given the existence of the Internet and cellphones, there are no problems whatsoever in making oneself clear without significantly increasing the risk of capture.

A further, fatal flaw of O'Neill's consists in her completely confused assumptions about the relationship between fear and uncertainty. She is at pains to make a distinction between terrorists (whom she deems to be the worst enemies of states, although one might more reasonably assume that the worst enemies of states are other states) and "the non-terrorist states and governments they oppose".[21] She claims:

The difference lies in the relatively slight use that governments make of strategies for spreading fear and terror, in their reliance on known law and known penalties, rather than cryptic menace and the spread of fear.... Terrorist speech by its very nature must be elliptical. Those who use it for the most part hide its true nature and import.... Their strategy is to spread uncertainty and ambiguity, and to create a level of fear that serves their ultimate objectives, without risking exposure. By contrast, governments—even bad governments—can communicate what the law requires and the penalties violators will face, in ways that allow those who live under law to form reliable expectations and to act with prudence to avoid those penalties. Even where laws are bad and government is harsh, those who live under law can aim to stay on the right side of it, and so will not face the levels and form of fear and uncertainty created in those whom terrorists target.[22]

The question that suggests itself is this: Why should *certain* death frighten me *less* than the mere *un*certainty as to whether I will live still longer? Let us say a bad government known for its effectiveness in carrying out its threats clearly communicates that it will kill everyone who opposes it. Is that clear communication likely to instil *less* fear in its opponents than the veiled communication of a tiny terrorist organization that it might kill some people if they do not watch out? I do not think so! And while it might be true that those who stay on the right side of the harsh government's deadly anti-opposition laws might be able to live more or less free of the fear of being killed by the government, this is obviously not so for those who decide to continue to oppose the government. They will definitely experience incomparably higher levels of fear than the (highly potential) targets of subnational terrorists. (Besides, as I have already said, more often than not the demands of terrorists are clear enough to enable people to stay on the safe side of these demands, too.) Moreover, this holds not only for harsh governments but also for milder ones. They will instil more fear in those who continue breaking certain laws than terrorist organizations are normally able to instil in those who do not comply with their demands.

At this point one could simply acknowledge the (quite obvious) fact that uncertain punishment or suffering does not instil more fear than more or less certain punishment or suffering, but still claim that the "veiled" character of the threats and the attempt to create uncertainty is a defining characteristic of terrorism. Then, however, one would like to know why. O'Neill's description of the behaviour of groups which are typically terrorist is empirically wrong and therefore does not help. Besides, making the "veiled" character of the threats and the attempt to create uncertainty a defining characteristic of terrorism would have extremely weird implications. Normally, the harsh state in my example would count as terrorist because it kills off all opponents it gets its hands on (including non-combatants) and tries to intimidate the rest of the population into desisting from opposition. However, on O'Neill's model this strategy of the state would not be terrorist at all, because the threat is not veiled and the killing not uncertain enough. If the state, however, adopted the appropriate speech act in its legislation ("Unsavoury elements might properly be dealt with by the security agencies") and then started to kill off some opponents, the state would become terrorist, whereas it was not so before. This implication shows quite clearly, in my view, the absurdity of O'Neill's premise.

Thus, Coady is quite right in not including the intention of spreading terror or fear, or fear induced by uncertainty-creating veiled threats, in his definition of terrorism. As Thomas C. Schelling or Annette C. Baier (among others) remark, the motivation behind terrorist acts such as attacks on civilian skyscrapers or aeroplanes can lie, for example, in the fact that these acts strengthen the enduring will of a group or direct the attention of the world to a certain problem by means of a violent provocative spectacle or of "shock".[23]

Waldron, Held and O'Neill do not think that the attack on non-combatants is a defining characteristic of terrorism. However, they attack that criterion not so much head-on as by way of collateral damage, as it were, of their emphasis on terror, fear and uncertainty. Since this emphasis is, as we just saw, rather misplaced, the criterion remains unscathed. J. Angelo Corlett, however, does attack it head-on. His objection is "that sneaking the harming of non-combatants or innocents into the definition of 'terrorism'... *begs the moral questions* against terrorism".[24] For "what possible role", then, "can terrorism have in society besides a negative one?"[25]

Actually, the criterion does *not* beg the moral question. Corlett even acknowledges that much on the next page.[26] This, however, does not keep him from repeatedly complaining that people like Coady or Primoratz "unwarrantedly sneak into the construal of terrorism ... a feature which is obviously (by the lights of most) either morally problematic or unjustified".[27] In fact, he *claims* that the attacks on military targets can constitute terrorism, but he does not show it. Rather, it seems that he uncritically accepts certain newspaper notions of terrorism. The definition he comes up with, by the way, implies that the enforcement of penal law is terrorism, too.[28] Be that as it may, while he reproaches Coady, Primoratz and many others for begging the question, he is begging the question himself. For why should the criterion of the attack on non-combatants have to be *sneaked in*?

Consider the case of rape. One definition that would suggest itself is that to rape a person is to force this person with violence or severe threats of violence to have sexual intercourse with one. Whatever else one might object to in this definition, it is hardly a valid objection to say that sneaking into the definition a feature that in the view of most people is morally problematic (i.e. forcing a person with violence or severe threats of violence to have sex with one) is to beg the question against rape and to obscure the positive role rape could play in our society. Rather, that feature belongs to the nature of rape. Or consider the case of genocide. Of course, defining genocide in such a way that it includes the intentional annihilation of a large part of a people or ethnic group makes genocide morally problematic and hinders us from seeing the positive role genocide could play in society. That, however, says very little against the correctness of the definition. The same holds for Corlett's remarks on Coady's definition. Apart from the invalid claim that Coady begs the question, he has nothing to offer against Coady's definition.

However, although Coady's definition is invaluable as a starting point, it does have shortcomings. For one, it is not clear why there should be only political, and not criminal, terrorism.[29] If someone blackmails a state by blowing up hospitals and by threatening to continue to do so unless he receives a certain large amount of money, there is no reason why this should not be called "terrorism". Second, it seems to be a decisive characteristic of terrorism that the immediate victims of its violence are not the only or the principal addressees of its further effects (e.g. of intimidation). To put it in another way, if terrorism is a method of intimidation or blackmail, it is one that intimidates certain people (e.g. government members) by attacking *others* (e.g. some citizens). The people attacked can, of course, themselves be members of the target group of the intimidation, but if this group is identical with the attacked group, we are no longer dealing with terrorism.[30] When a bank robber threatens bank employees with his gun in order to get money from them, we would not call this a terrorist act. It is, rather, a typical bank robbery. As Igor Primoratz emphasizes, terrorism has "not one, but two targets: the immediate, direct target, which is of secondary importance, and the indirect target, which is really important".[31] Primoratz consequently defines terrorism as

the deliberate use of violence, or the threat of its use, against innocent people, with the aim of intimidating *some other people* into a course of action they otherwise would not take.[32]

David Rodin thinks that double targeting and hence the attempt to affect in some way an indirect target is not an essential feature of terrorism. His definition of terrorism is this:

[T]errorism is the deliberate, negligent, or reckless use of force against noncombatants, by state or nonstate actors for ideological ends and in the absence of a substantively just legal process.[33]

However, the double structure seems to be an important part of our linguistic intuitions with regard to the term "terrorism". In particular, Rodin's definition cannot, as it should, distinguish terrorism from pure genocide. Of course, genocide *can* be terrorist, for example, when it is used to frighten off the surviving part of the targeted population (making it leave a contended territory). But to call a *pure* genocide terrorism, a genocide which has no other purpose than to exterminate the whole targeted population, seems odd. Also, any ideologically motivated euthanasia, silently carried out in some hospitals, would be "terrorist" on Rodin's account. Finally, a sect committing suicide for ideological reasons somewhere in the South American jungle would thereby be terrorist. In my view, these implications of Rodin's definition call for its rejection.

However, there is yet a further feature of terrorism. Would we speak of terrorism in the case of a kidnapping when other people, for example the relatives of the kidnapped person, are being blackmailed to pay ransom? Obviously not. So there is still something missing. An isolated act of intimidation of third parties by an attack on innocents (or by a threat against innocents) is not sufficient; nor even is a series of attacks. Rather, in my view, the decisive criterion here is this: In *what*, exactly, does the threat consist? If, in a series of kidnappings, the relatives are blackmailed each time to pay money because otherwise the kidnapped person will be killed (see Sicily), we are dealing with a case of serial crime, not with terrorism. The situation changes, however, when the group or family of which all the kidnapped persons are, as we are assuming here, members, is blackmailed to pay money *because otherwise the series of kidnappings will continue.* Let us consider yet another example: A sniper threatens a city with the claim that he will kill some inhabitants if he is not given a certain amount of money. He receives the money. In the following months he repeats the blackmail. He again receives the money (or not, with the result that he carries out his threat). And so on. This is simply repeated blackmail or a series of blackmails. On the other hand, if the blackmailer threatens to kill an inhabitant every month unless he is paid a certain amount of money (and acts accordingly because otherwise his threat would become less credible), this indeed is terrorism.[34] Of course, our linguistic intuitions in these areas are not crystal clear, since the term "terrorism" is, not least for propaganda reasons, used in many ways. It is clear, however, that terrorism has to be distinguished from mere blackmail, irrespective of whether the latter has a political or mere financial thrust. The difference is, I propose, that terrorism threatens with itself, as it were. The mere blackmailer says, perhaps even repeatedly: "If you don't do what I tell you, I will shoot someone." The terrorist says: "If you don't do what I tell you, I will kill *again and again.*" This threat, of course, must also be credible in order to allow us to speak of terrorism (instead of just a bad joke), and this requires that it be carried out or emphasized in some other way. This carrying out or emphasis are of course themselves implicit threats. Thus, terrorism is the credible threat of repeated attacks on innocents. This does not exclude the possibility of one-off acts of terrorism: one violent act, without follow-ups, can still make a threat of *repeated* violent acts credible. However, a one-off act of violence can be called terrorist only if it is a part of such a strategy that threatens more than one act of violence.[35] Incidentally, this also corresponds to the origin of the words "terrorism" and "terror" in the French "*régime de la terreur*", the rule of terror of the Jacobins after the French Revolution.

A third problem with Coady's definition is his talk of "non-combatants" instead of "innocents". The two groups are not identical. An entrepreneur who produces the gas for a genocide is not a combatant, at least not according to the laws of armed conflict. However, he is definitely not innocent, and there seems to be nothing particularly fishy about targeting him. The reason for this is that through his actions he has made himself *liable* to attack by those who want to stop the genocide. I can see no sufficient reason why such an attack on a civilian or non-combatant who clearly contributes to a grave crime should be called *terrorist*. This is even so when such an attack is carried out not only to eliminate the target but also to frighten off other would-be suppliers of deadly gas for the genocide. The term "terrorist" has, as I have already pointed out, a very negative connotation. Therefore, we should not use it for things that are not particularly negative—that would only be misleading. Killing innocents *is* very bad. It might still be justified under certain conditions, but such a justification does not change the fact that in an act of terrorism the *rights of those innocents who should not be attacked are violated*. It only means that in some dire circumstances certain rights violations can be justified as the lesser evil. (To be sure, Coady would point out that he uses the term "combatant" for someone who is "engaged in prosecuting an attack upon us or others or engaged in some similar project involving the infliction of gross injustice".[36] The entrepreneur producing poison gas for a genocide would clearly fall under this description. However, while Coady is on the right track, he still uses a misleading expression. "Combatant" is simply too closely tied to its interpretation within the laws of armed conflict—and there the poison gas producer would not be a combatant, for he does not produce it as a weapon of war—to be used in the way Coady does without becoming misleading.)

In accordance with these remarks, I propose the following definition of terrorism and terrorist acts:

Terrorism is the strategy of influencing the behaviour, perceptions, beliefs or attitudes of others than the immediate victims or targets of its violence by the threat, made credible by a corresponding act or series of acts, of the repeated killing or severe harming of innocents or the repeated destruction or severe harming of their property. *Terrorist acts* are such severe attacks on innocents or their property that are part of such a strategy.

As stated previously, the others who are to be influenced by the terrorist's violence can also be the terrorist's own followers or clients, whose enduring will the terrorist seeks to strengthen.[37] Thus, the aim need not necessarily be the intimidation of someone.

Nevertheless, we still usually assume that, at least in the *paradigmatic* case of terrorism, not only the violence against innocents but also the attempt at intimidation are defining characteristics; and it suggests itself to begin the ethical analysis of terrorism with such paradigmatic cases of terrorist acts. Georg Meggle calls them terrorist acts in the "strong sense" and defines them as "acts in which purposes are (attempted to be) brought about by means of terror induced by violence committed against some innocents".[38] In contrast to Coady's definition, here violence against innocents includes not only that violence which chooses innocents as a direct target, but also such violence which takes the harming of innocents into account and accepts the possibility of making them victims. In this context, Meggle speaks of "strongly reprehensible collateral damage".[39]

Can terrorism, thus defined, ever be justified? Meggle denies this, which leads him to condemn both the attack on the World Trade Center and the "Counter-Terror" measures of the United States in Afghanistan. What eludes him, however, is this: according to his own definition of terrorism, those legislators who employ a system of justice with penal and process law in order that they may punish criminals and *deter* delinquents from committing crimes commit thereby themselves a terrorist act in the strong sense. For even if they take precautions to minimize the danger of killing innocents by their acts, they know very well that this danger can never be completely removed, and what is more, they know that innocents will ever and again be affected. This risk—the risk of "strongly reprehensible collateral damage", to use Meggle's own terms—is one which such legislators clearly take. The applicability of Meggle's definition to a system of criminal justice does not necessarily show that this definition is faulty, however. As Agnes Heller has ascertained: "Terror does not originate in totalitarianism. Rather, it has its origin in the principal of deterrence..., which has also been introduced in the legal procedures of democracies."[40] But since it is counter-intuitive to deem such acts of positing penal law as per se morally contemptible, Meggle's thesis on the categorical illegitimacy of ("strong") terrorism remains unconvincing.

In fact, the analogy with a system of criminal law for punishment and deterrence perhaps opens a line of argument for the justification of terrorism, where possible. Let us suppose, for example, that the attack on the World Trade Center was an act of punishment for the policy of Israel and the United States toward the Palestinians. (In the United States there recently appeared a collection of essays from US dissidents; on the cover of the book the remains of the World Trade Center are pictured, and in the foreground we read: "A Just Response".) Human rights organizations such as Human Rights Watch have made reference to the fact that civilians have been (and continue to be) targeted in diverse Israeli military actions. In this sense, we are indeed dealing with Israeli state terrorism, which is also supported by the United States, and to which we may add the non-state terrorism of Israeli settlers. This Israeli-American terrorism has caused more casualties than all the Arab strikes of retaliation taken together. But would this justify a retaliatory strike on the World Trade Center, assuming that the attack really was such a strike? Even if one were to assign many of the victims a partial responsibility for US policy in the Middle East—the United States is, after all, a democracy—their responsibility could hardly be large enough to warrant the death penalty. Nevertheless, one could argue—in the sense of Meggle's definition of terrorism—that the victims of the attack on the World Trade Center are meant only as a kind of means: to punish either all Americans and Europeans, or at least as many as possible, namely by means of a growing feeling of fear and uncertainty. Surely innocents were also affected (e.g. people who were engaged in the struggle for the rights of the Palestinians) and guilty parties were punished too severely, but this is a risk which one also takes in a system of penal and criminal law with the principle of deterrence. The difference between the two would no longer be one of principle, but would rather lie in the dimensions and appropriateness of the attack. If, as certain Israeli and US governments have believed and continue to believe, those so-called acts of retaliation by the Israeli army which terrorized the entire Palestinian population are justified; if Clinton's strike against Sudan—which, according to the report of the German ambassador there, caused thousands of deaths—is justified; or even if the sanctions against Iraq are justified, though they have caused some half million civilian deaths, of which half have been those of children; if all these acts are justified, it is not at all clear why the attack on the World Trade Center should not be justified, if it is in fact understood as an act of retaliation as well.

Here one might object that both Israeli and Arab terrorism are illegitimate and that both are very well to be distinguished in principle from criminal and penal law, to the degree that the latter does not *intend* to affect innocent victims, but rather only *takes them into account*. This, however, is of course nothing but an appeal to the doctrine of double effect, the incorrectness of which has already been demonstrated above. The morally relevant difference does not, as I have said, lie in the question as to whether someone employs the death of innocents as a means to his ends or foresees it as a consequence, but rather whether the person in question welcomes the death of the innocents or regrets it. This is not a difference between terrorists on the one hand and legislators on the other; it is rather one between different kinds of legislators and terrorists.

Yet there is a difference between the positing of penal law, on the one hand, and terrorism, on the other hand.[41] In fact, we have already come to know this difference, namely in the form of the above example of a spy who kills the innocent wives of some Nazi bosses in order to demoralize these Nazis.[42] I said that a double injustice lies in such an act: the women suffer something they do not deserve, while one lets the aggressors, the actual targets of the attack, get away with their lives. What human beings deserve or do not deserve relative to one another and, on the other hand, do or do not get is, after all, a central aspect for our sense of justice. Although, so

I argued, the death of the latter might appear proportionate if one considers the events under the aspect of what was achieved through it, namely their husbands' unsuitability for war, it nevertheless remains disproportionate under the aspect just described.

However, it should be clear that this difference, as important as it may be, is by no means a guarantee for the disproportionality of an attack on innocents for the sake of a demoralization or deterrence or intimidation of certain groups. (It does not mean, either, that the line of action taken by the Americans and British in Afghanistan was non-terrorist. Admiral Sir Michael Boyce explained during the war that bombing would continue "until the people of the country themselves recognise that this is going to go on until they get the leadership changed".[43] This is still a terrorist strategy as defined by our above definition, that is, even if we do not follow Meggle in regarding the causation of "highly imputable collateral damages" as in itself terrorist.) Rather, it merely enters the proportionality considerations as a trump. Such trumps, like rights, can in sufficiently extreme situations be overridden by utilitarian considerations, as has already been emphasized here several times against absolutist views. But the justificational force lies then in the extreme situation, not in the alleged symmetry between terrorism and penal law. We will return to justification by an extreme situation in a moment. First, however, another proposal for a justification of terrorism must be considered. It comes from Held:

It seems reasonable, I think, that on grounds of justice, it is better to equalize rights violations in a transition to bring an end to rights violations than it is to subject a given group that has already suffered extensive rights violations to continued such violations, if the degree of severity of the two violations is similar. . . . If we must have rights violations, a more equitable distribution of such violations is better than a less equitable distribution.[44]

The attack on non-combatants would be legitimized here by means of reference to *groups* as recipients of a supposedly just distribution of rights violations. Since Held explicitly understands this strategy of legitimization as based on rights and not on utility, a question from the logical point of view seems to arise itself right away: How can one have recourse to rights in order to legitimize their infraction? This is a difficulty which Held could solve simply by giving a more carefully worded version of her argument. However, it is quite appropriate, especially in light of certain extreme situations, to rethink the logic of rights. Rights violations can be justified.[45] Be that as it may, one may readily assume that a position such as Held represents would not be unattractive for many members of groups which fall victim to oppression and rights violations. The concept of "poetic justice" plays a certain role here. The ethnologist James C. Scott reported the reaction of many black people to the sinking of the *Titanic*:

The drowning of large numbers of wealthy and powerful whites . . . in their finery aboard a ship that was said to be unsinkable seemed like a stroke of poetic justice to many blacks. . . . "Official" songs about the loss of the *Titanic* were sung ironically ("It was *saaad* when the great ship went down").[46]

Naturally, similar reactions could be seen in wake the of the destruction of the World Trade Center—and in fact, such reactions are indeed natural. In reaction to them, certain persons, especially in the German and American press, pointed the moral finger and condemned the lack of compassion on the part of many in the Arab world (the level of compassion in a significant portion of the Latin-American population was not much greater, but this was a fact concerning which the established press chose to keep silent). Here another injustice is to be found: the oppressed not only have to bear an unequal distribution of rights violations, one also demands of them more compassion for those who profit from this unequal distribution than the privileged are required to show for the oppressed. Thus Ron Hirschbein remarks on public opinion in the United States during the second Gulf War:

There was no public outcry, for example, when the popular press cited the conclusion of a Harvard Medical School study: 75,000 Iraqi children would die due to the destruction of the Iraqi infrastructure. The civic celebration continued as Bush's popularity soared.[47]

Yet, though such a lack of compassion in the public opinion of the United States was manifest, moral fingers were pointed neither there nor in Germany. Apparently, Americans who do not let the death of 75,000 children rain on the parade for their bombs are more acceptable than Arabs who, in view of 3,000 American casualties, are glad that misfortune hit the other side for a change. Such discrepancies understandably increase the willingness of oppressed peoples to see whole groups as enemies and thus to have recourse to an argumentative strategy such as Held's.

Igor Primoratz, however, objects to Held's argument:

> Faced with the prospect of being killed or maimed on the grounds of this ... justification, might I not draw on Nozick's view of rights, and say that I am a person in my own right, that my life is the only life I have and all I have, and that nobody may take it away, nor ruin it by making me a cripple, for the sake of, and subsequently more general respect for, the right to life and bodily security within a group of people? ... The value and significance of my life is not derived from my membership in a group. Nobody may sacrifice it to the group.[48]

On the other hand, Primoratz thinks it legitimate if an artillery unit fires at a village and hence kills innocents, as long as it meets the precondition that it fulfils the requirements of the doctrine of double effect, that is, "those casualties were unintended, inevitable, reduced to a minimum, and proportionate to the military aim achieved".[49] Quite apart from the fact that the doctrine of double effect is simply wrong, it is also rather one-sided for Primoratz to put himself into the role of the victim when he is dealing with terrorism, but not to do so when he is dealing with the bombing of villages by the military. For the victim of such a bombing could say the following:

> Faced with the prospect of being killed or maimed on the grounds of the doctrine of double effect (or on the grounds of someone else's presumably having a positive duty to do this to me), might I not draw on Nozick's view of rights, and say that I am a person in my own right, that my life is the only life I have and all I have, and that nobody may take it away, nor ruin it by making me a cripple, for the sake of achieving a military aim, probably of killing other people (namely soldiers). The value and significance of my life is not derived from my being near to some group of soldiers. Nobody may sacrifice it in killing such a group.

Here the life of the complainer is even sacrificed in order to make other people *worse* off (namely, to kill them). As long as these people are not aggressors (but soldiers of the just side), there is, one would suppose, an even stronger reason to complain than in the case in which one's death at least results in something good.

Thus, if, as Primoratz holds, one of the two things is legitimate—the Heldian terrorism or the Primoratzian artillery fire—it will be the Heldian terrorism.

Nevertheless, Held's argument is wrong. Its point is, in contrast to purely consequentialist or utilitarian arguments, to play rights off against rights. (This, by the way, is also done by the above argument that appeals to an analogy between certain terrorist acts and the positing of penal law.) Mere interests can hardly override a right. Conflicting rights can do this much more easily, as the conflict between the right to attack an aggressor and the right of an innocent (who gets in the line of fire) to life shows (of course, the right to attack an aggressor is a very strong right).[50] But the Achilles heel of Held's argument is precisely that the postulated right to an equalization of violence risks or rights violations does not exist in the way which is relevant here. The example given by Held is in more than one respect misleading:

The right to personal security, of freedom from unlawful attack, can be fully recognized as a right in a given legal community, and yet of course some assault will occur. The community's way of trying to assure respect for such rights is likely to include the deployment of police forces. But if almost all the police forces are deployed in high-income white neighborhoods and almost none in low-income black neighborhoods, ... we can judge without great difficulty that the deployment is unfair.[51]

This is correct, but what she has to show is not the injustice of these unequal risks induced by the unjust distribution of the police forces, but rather that the order described in the example is less just than one in which some poor blacks (or their helpers) go over to the rich whites in order to equalize the risk of being the victim of violence by killing some of them. Indeed, this *can* be more just, namely in circumstances in which the whites themselves have brought about this unjust distribution of police forces. Then they are *aggressors*, they *violate the rights* of the blacks. Consequently, however, they are not innocent any more; but it is with an attack on innocents that we are supposed to be dealing here. Second, the example of the distribution of existing police forces does not do justice to the fact that, in the case of the distribution of rights violations, there is no determined quantity of such violations such that in order to distribute them we only have to select the victims who will receive them. If it is a determined fact that each year one thousand murders are committed and one is forced to distribute them in some way, it would probably be best to let a lottery decide (provided, of course, that one does not know who the murderers will be). Thus, a distribution which would exempt all whites from the role of the victim would certainly be unjust. In the face of such a distribution it would seem justified that the blacks obvert part of the violence to the whites, even if the whites themselves are completely innocent of the manipulation. In fact, however, the "distribution" of rights violations is not a zero sum game. This means that if the blacks march off to kill some whites, they do not thereby redistribute "pre-existing" acts of violence, but they produce new ones. While it may be just to distribute a fixed total suffering or total rights violations burden equally on all shoulders, it is rather unjust to equalize the suffering of one innocent by making the other innocents suffer, too. "If one group is having a bad time, the others shall also have a bad time"—this does not appear to be a particularly commendable principle of justice. If to this someone objects that Held does not want to stop with a graver, but more equally distributed, burden of suffering and rights violations, that person misunderstands her argument. For the decisive point is *how* the redistribution—also against innocents—is to be justified. After all, she does not want to justify it with an appeal to a better end result—this would be a utilitarian or consequentialist argument—but with an appeal to distributive justice. She claims that the redistributive measures are not only conducive to a certain ideal state, but above all *more just.* And for the reason given this claim is not correct. Moreover, there is still a third reason, which consists in the difficulty of identifying a suitable "receiver group" for the redistribution of the rights viola-tions. For let us assume that Joe, Jim and Jill (group 1) as well as Frank, Fred and Fran (group 2) live in the poor neighbourhood, while Bob, Bill and Berta (group 3) live in the rich one. Let us further assume that the members of group 1 have already been robbed and bear a high risk of being robbed again, while this is not true for the members of groups 2 and 3. (Frank and Fred are monks, Fran is a nun, and this is respected by the criminals in the neighbourhood as sufficient reason not to assault them, apart from the fact that they do

not have any valuables anyway.) Why, now, should the redistribution
of rights violations or of risks of becoming a victim of violence
proceed from group 1 to group 3—which is probably what Held has
in mind—instead of proceeding from group 1 to group 2? Again, one
cannot argue that the latter redistribution may lead to an absolute
lowering of the rate of rights violations because this, as already
mentioned, would not be a rights-based argument. Montague's
selection principle[52] does not function either, for *ex hypothesi* the
members of group 3 are innocents. Moreover, group 2 does not profit
less from the unequal distribution than group 3—let alone that
someone's *innocent* profiting is hardly a sufficient reason to violate
his rights.

But what happens if the receiver group is *not* innocent? Well, one
could say, then we are not dealing with terrorism any more. This
is a correct observation. It has, however, the important consequence
that many acts that are hastily called "terrorism" and condemned as
such are not terrorism at all. Just because certain human beings are
civilians does not mean that they are automatically innocent. They
may, as we saw above,[53] still be engaged in an attempt to destroy
or otherwise severely harm you. Besides, according to Montague's
selection principle, they are not only legitimate targets for the redistribution of harm when they attempt at a given moment to cause such
harms, but also when they are responsible for the occurrence of a
certain harm.[54] A present attack or a present undertaking which
would lead to harm is not even necessary. An example given by Jeff
McMahan may illustrate this again:

Suppose there is a group of your enemies who wish you to be killed,
since they will profit from your death. They build a device that can be
programmed to transmit irresistible commands to a person through a
receiver implanted in his brain. Once programmed and activated the device
requires no further guidance or intervention. Your enemies then kidnap an
innocent person, install the implant in his brain, . . . and activate the [con-
trolling] device. . . . Your only recourse [to save yourself], other than killing
the innocent pursuer, is to coerce your enemies to deactivate or reveal the
location of the device. You soon realize, however, that the only way to do this
is to begin killing them, one by one, until one of them is sufficiently
intimidated to tell you where the device is located. . . . Assuming that killing
the enemies would be equally effective in averting the threat and other things

are equal, it is clearly morally preferable to kill the enemies—and to kill as many of them as necessary—rather than to kill the innocent pursuer.[55]

McMahan is certainly correct. Now, the important point with this example is that the control device was activated in the past. The group of enemies is at the moment neither attacking nor supporting an attack, nor preparing one. Rather, the endangered person is endangered by the consequences of an already *past* act. Nevertheless, he is obviously justified to deviate the harm—death—to those who are responsible for it. Let us now turn to another similar case. In Israel, a democracy, the people vote with a large majority for a presumed war criminal, terrorist, militarist and racist, namely for Ariel Sharon. Sharon is comparable here with the control device in McMahan's example. Once such a person is president, the people do not need to demand brutality and crimes against the Palestinians—he will do this of his own accord, which is precisely the reason why the Israelis trustingly elected him. We are dealing here with a case of hired murder, hired mutilation and hired deprivation of liberty. Israelis who voted for Sharon are therefore as guilty for the crimes he commits against the Palestinians as the enemies in McMahan's example are for the persecution of the threatened person. If, by killing them one by one, one could cause them to end the criminal Israeli policies against Palestine and to recognize the human rights of Palestinians and their right to self-determination (e.g. by voting for an adequate president), this would be justified. Of course, in attacks against civilians innocents would be killed, too—e.g. Israelis who have emphatically spoken up for the rights of Palestinians. But these deaths of innocents would be "collateral damages"—they would occur in the course of the attack on an aggressor (on the Israelis who voted for Sharon). Direct attacks on school busses, kindergartens or similar targets, however, would still be terrorist attacks, because the children did not vote for Sharon.

Naturally, one might doubt whether the premise (the "if" clause) of this justification is fulfilled. And this is indeed doubtful. There are good reasons to assume that the Palestinians do more harm than good to their cause by their attacks on civilians. However, with the said premise I kept completely to McMahan's interpretation. But, in fact, I would contradict him with regard to a decisive point:

I would be legitimized to kill the enemies one by one even if I knew with certainty that, in the end, I could not escape the persecutor with the implant.[56] This is simply an application of my liberal right to punish aggressors (if there is no superior punishing power, or if it neglects its duties or is not able to meet them in this case, and my right to punish overrides my duty to abstain from private justice because of the gravity of the crime). On the other hand, one must emphasize that it is illicit to give the punishment of the guilty priority to the protection of innocents. Since attacks on civilians in some coffee houses will inevitably also kill innocents, probabilities of success remain relevant.[57] The same holds, of course, for proportionality and last resort. Depending on the assessments which a responsible calculation will yield here, the Palestinian attacks on Israeli voters are either justified or not. Even if they are not justified, however, they would, for the reasons mentioned, not be terrorist.

A further strategy for the legitimization of terrorism may be developed from considerations forwarded by Michael Walzer, though very much against his intentions. He thinks that subnational terrorism is neither to be legitimized, nor to be excused. In accordance with this position is the manifesto signed by fifty-eight scholars in the United States, in which we read that "no appeal to the merits or demerits of specific foreign policies can ever justify... the mass slaughter of innocent persons".[58] Yet, in his book *Just and Unjust Wars*, he considers the mistakes committed by the German government as sufficient justification for the terror bombing of German cities (Walzer himself uses this term). Supposedly, German policy threatened the survival and freedom of the political community of Britain in such a way as to justify this use of the only potent offensive weapon which the British possessed in 1940 and 1941.[59] Walzer is "inclined", as he says, to accept this justification not only in the face of Nazi-like threats against the whole of humanity:

Can soldiers and statesmen override the rights of innocent people for the sake of their own political community? I am inclined to answer this question affirmatively, though not without hesitation and worry.[60]

Walzer's further remarks and his very high esteem of political communities,[61] however, demonstrate that these worries are somewhat limited:

[T]he survival and freedom of political communities—whose members share a way of life, developed by their ancestors, to be passed on to their children—are the highest values of international society.[62]

Therefore, Andrew Valls, who criticizes Walzer's double moral standard, asks the obvious question:

But why is it that the territorial integrity and political independence of, say, Britain, justify the resort to... violence that targets civilians—but the right of self-determination of a stateless nation never does?[63]

Apparently there is no reason for this, especially since Walzer explicitly deduces the rights of states from those of communities, and the rights of these from those of individuals.[64]

Let me adduce two further examples for the justificatory force of a state of emergency. Imagine a head of household whose family is kidnapped by slave traders. A direct attack on them would be doomed to failure because of the superior weapons technology of the slave traders. For the father there is no other possibility to save his family than to use an opportunity to kidnap the innocent daughter of the leader of the slave traders, and to threaten to kill her if his family is not released. Can he really be blamed for the calculated violence against an innocent, or do the slave traders bear the responsibility for the escalation? In order to eliminate any doubts: yes, he violates the rights of the innocent daughter by kidnapping her, and yes, he makes himself guilty. But, in my view, he does not bear the brunt of the guilt. His positive duties towards his family may override, in this case, the negative duties against the leader's daughter. It would be a justified, or at least an excusable, action.

Let us further imagine the chief of a tribal association, which is also continuously raided by slave traders. Direct resistance against the slave traders is hopeless because of their superiority in terms of weapons technology. As a consequence, the chief resorts to employing reprisals against civilians. After every abduction raid by the slave traders, he dispatches some warriors and has them kill a certain number of the relatives of the slave traders. Here, too, we are dealing with a justifying emergency. Whoever is only able to condemn attacks on innocents even in such cases—in which one's only chance of saving many other innocents with whom one has ties is precisely to attack a smaller number of innocents whose ties are with the enemy side—and is unable to see here a possible justification or at least an excuse: such a person does not so much demonstrate a Kantian loyalty to principles, but an appalling lack of empathy for the desperation of those who suffer from the arbitrariness and brutality of the strong.

"Arbitrariness and brutality of the strong" is, to be sure, the decisive cue. I have argued above that the rule-utilitarian justification for the principle of non-combatant immunity does not permit violating this principle in a certain situation only because thereby more, and be it even many more, innocent people can be saved *in this situation* than by abiding to the principle. Rather, the further effects of the violation of the principle must also be considered. As the example of the violation, and resulting further disregard, of this principle at the hands of the Allies in the Second World War shows, in most cases following such a rule, with the attendant recognition and strengthening of the rule which contribute to the rule's also being followed in the future, serves human utility better than violating the rule.[65] If Truman had refrained from using atom bombs, if he had justified not dropping the bomb on the basis of a respect for the immunity of non-combatants, and had pleaded earnestly for such a principle after the war, if Truman had done all this, it might have made an impression on the US military so deep that it would have retreated rather than carry out a campaign against civilians in Vietnam, and perhaps would never have entered the conflict in the first place. That would have spared the lives of 58,000 US soldiers, about one million Vietnamese soldiers and at least two million Vietnamese civilians. Instead, we are dealing today with a US military (and, apparently, a majority of US citizens) that would rather kill a hundred civilians than risk the life of a single soldier of their own. So much for my argument from above.

It is, however, decisive to see that "most cases" do not comprise the one in which the civilians of a weak people are systematically attacked by a strong aggressor, and where there is no other possibility to stop these attacks than the counter-attack on the innocent civilians on the other side. This violation of the rule, to wit, by no means leads to greater consequential damages than non-violation. As paradoxical as it may sound, just the opposite seems to be the case. If strong states are safe from severe reprisals following upon their attacks on civilians—and this is obviously the case when the only severe reprisal of which the opposing side remains capable consists of attacking the innocents of the aggressor side, but the opposing side does not use this form of reprisal—then these strong states have, as long as attacks on civilians serve their purposes, no reason to refrain from them. From this it follows that such a continuous abstention of weak communities from reacting against the attack on their civilians with the only strategy still available to them gives the aggressors a free hand. Accordingly, the weak communities' abstaining from the counter-attack on civilians is likely to increase, in future, the overall number of killed innocents or the scale of the deprivation of liberty. This does not lead to the rule "If a community can protect a large number of their innocents from an aggressor only by attacking a smaller number of the innocents of the aggressor, then this is admissible", but rather to the rule "If a community can protect a large number of their innocents from an aggressor only by attacking a smaller number of the innocents of the aggressor, then this is admissible *provided that it is not to be expected that a group of aggressors sufficiently large for the purposes of deterrence will be punished for their attacks*". That a rejection of *this* principle cannot be justified in rule-utilitarian terms while its acceptance can, may already easily be seen by the italicized subordinate clause alone. It is also obvious that strong states confronted with weak states will hardly come into the situation described by the if clause and the provided clause. They may have recourse to other countermeasures and reprisals, up to and including war crime tribunals.

We may, then, reach the following conclusions. Whoever seeks to legitimize certain *particular* acts of terrorism carries the burden of proof, for the protection of innocents is indeed an extraordinarily precious right and legal good. To outweigh this right in any particular situation there must be very good and very carefully examined reasons. On the other hand, whoever claims that terrorism can *never* be justified also carries the burden of proof, as shown by the fundamental disposability of such legitimization strategies as the ones just outlined. This claim—that terrorism is never justified—would only be valid under the ethical premise that direct attack on civilians in acceptance of risking the lives of innocent victims is *absolutely* forbidden. Sad to say, such a premise is hardly plausible in the context of an ethics of responsibility; this premise is also rejected by the great majority of those who now loudly denounce terrorism as absolutely evil and bad. But, when such persons want to justify the terrorism which they think is good, they often have recourse to one or the other of the patterns of argumentation described above, often in combination. Of course they do not call it terrorism—they may call it a "war against terror", as in the case of the massive bombing in Afghanistan or Clinton's rocket strike in Sudan, or they may also call it a "war-shortening measure", as in the case of the use of atomic bombs in Hiroshima and Nagasaki.

A first result of these considerations is that the inference from the terrorist character of an attack to its illegitimacy is not valid. At best, the inference of the probability of the act's illegitimacy would be valid. But this in turn means that, according to the criteria of just war, if a state falls victim to a terrorist attack, it must first examine the reasons motivating the attack, and it certainly cannot dismiss out of hand the question of motivation as irrelevant before it claims the right to take a bellicose countermeasure. Even if this examination is brought to the conclusion that the attack was illegitimate, it still opens the possibility to recognize that the perpetrators did not act out of purely evil intentions, but rather more probably out of desperation—a desperation for which the victim is perhaps not completely unaccountable. This recognition could possibly lead to a certain amount of moderation in the application of countermeasures. Herein lies precisely the purpose and meaning of a theory of just war (or at least, it should do so today): to limit war, and not to promote self-justice and grant open warrants to destroy.

A second, substantial conclusion of these considerations results from the nature of the patterns of justification outlined. As previously mentioned, these are also used by the apologists for state terrorism. However, these patterns do not fail to recognize the validity of proportionality or just measure, and of the probability of success, as criteria in the judgement of the justification of an act of violence. It is not only, but also, for this reason that the constraints of these schemes are not just difficult to fulfil, but in fact, *more difficult for strong parties to fulfil than for weak ones*. Let us take the pattern of argument borrowed from Walzer as an example. The freedom of the political community of the Palestinians is not only threatened by Israel, but has in effect been prevented for some decades, and the creation of a Palestinian state—or even an autonomous region—has been foiled. The Palestinians are not standing with their backs to the wall; they are being smashed against it. But has the existence of Israel ever been threatened by the intifada or by the Palestinian Autonomy Authority, or would the existence of Israel be threatened by a Palestinian state? In consideration of the military might of Israel and its US ally, such a thought seems absolutely absurd. The idea that al-Qaeda or the Taliban could threaten the existence or freedom of the United States is just as absurd. A similar asymmetry is to be found in other patterns of argumentation, as could easily be shown. Nevertheless, most "serious" commentators tend to excuse the violence committed by the stronger party. (One could consider the mild, even positive, reactions to the US bombing of Tripoli in 1986 and of a pharmaceutical factory in 1998; the frequent retaliation measures directed against civilians in Israel; or the in famous sanctions against Iraq which, as previously mentioned, have already cost the lives of hundreds of thousands of civilians, half of which were children. At least the reactions to Israel's April 2002 attacks against the Palestinians give occasion for some glimmer of hope.) This is not only immoral and hypocritical, it defies all logic.

Terrorism is not at all the instrument of the weak, as is often claimed, but rather the routinely employed instrument of the strong, and usually only the final resort for the weak. (This is true for secular terrorism, not for that kind of terrorism which is motivated by apocalyptic visions such as may be found in the Aum Shinrikyo sect, certain racist militias in the United States and partially also in al-Qaeda.) As such a final instrument, terrorism is, to cite Baier, "a demonstration of this power to make resentment at exclusion felt".[66] We may add: resentment at exclusion from justice and freedom. Even if the United States were to succeed in its "war against terrorism" and were to annihilate all such terrorism which is neither promoted, supported or approved of by them, and thus were to remove the last resort of the excluded in their effort to put up some resistance—even then there would be only a little less violence in the world. There would certainly not be more justice. This "war against terrorism", waged by state terrorists and with terrorist means, does not have as its object universal values, but rather the attainment of undisputed power.

If strong states really want to fight subnational terrorism, there are only three legitimate and recommendable means at their disposal: the rejection of a double moral standard; the focused persecution of crime (insofar as the commission of a punishable crime—and not of an act of justifiable resistance—may be demonstrated); and, finally, the inclusion of the excluded.

Notes

CHAPTER 1

1. Coates (1997), p. 123.
2. Ibid., p. 124.
3. If at all, then it is the conversion of this statement which would be more plausible: "[I]t is our questioning of the agent's killing of the innocent that makes us question the legitimacy of the agent's authority, not the other way round." See Per Bauhn (2005), p. 126.
4. See Ch. 4.
5. Calhoun (2001a) emphatically advocates the view that the remaining criteria of just war theory are mere puppets on the strings of the criterion of "legitimate authority"—and hence of real such "authorities"—i.e. that just war theory is complete window-dressing. With regard to just war theory as a whole she is wrong; with regard to the account of Coates, she may be right.
6. Coates (1997), pp. 124f.
7. Ibid., p. 133.
8. Ibid., p. 125.
9. Cf. Johnson (1984), pp. 150–71.
10. Coates (1997), pp. 126f.
11. Ibid., p. 128.
12. Ibid., p. 129.
13. Ibid., p. 135.
14. Ibid., pp. 126f. and 129.
15. Cf. Thompson (2005), pp. 153f., for the dependence of Coates' criterion of legitimate authority on the criterion of *causa justa*, and Bauhn (2005), p. 126, for the dependence on the criterion of non-combatant immunity.
16. Thompson (2005), p. 153.
17. Ibid., p. 155.
18. Ibid., pp. 151f.
19. Ibid., p. 152.
20. Thompson (2002), p. 94.
21. Id. (2005), p. 159.
22. Ibid., pp. 156 and 158.

23. Ibid., p. 159.
24. Ibid., p. 155.
25. Ibid., pp. 156f.
26. Ibid., p. 155.
27. Ibid., p. 157.
28. Ibid., p. 158.
29. Coates (1997), pp. 134f.
30. Ibid., p. 140.
31. Locke (2002), pp. 401f., §§ 203–4. Locke's assessment follows a longer, and very good, justification.
32. Coates (1997), p. 127.
33. Ibid., p. 155.
34. Rodin claims that there are differences: "The state has an internal set of checks and balances, and in traditional just war theory the authority of the state comes from the fact that it is defending the community and is properly constituted to do so" (personal communication). And he thinks that I have to show that this argument is wrong. Well, first, in some states and communities the "set of checks and balances" pretty much boils down to the leader's conscience. And in fact, the deliberation process of a single individual may at times be much more balanced than a public political discourse infected with patriotism, or a decision process supported by a bureaucracy and advisory staff made up of yesmen and opportunists. More important, however, is that I do not claim that a state does not have a right to wage war; just war theorists, on the other hand, do claim that the individual doesn't have such a right. It seems, therefore, that the burden of proof is on them, not on me, especially since nowadays the professed political default position in academic circles, liberalism, claims that a state's rights derive from the individual, and not the other way round. What the "statists" or "communitarians" would have to show if they were to take up Rodin's line of argument is that a private decision process lacks certain qualities—in contradistinction to a community's decision process—which are *necessary* for becoming a legitimate authority. However, no one has shown anything of that sort; in fact, no one has even attempted to do so. Therefore, there is no reason—so far—to assume that an individual's authority to wage war cannot come from the fact that he defends his individuality and his individual rights. It is, instead, reasonable to assume that he can, and that he is legitimized to do so on grounds of precisely these rights, his rationality and his moral autonomy.
35. Vitoria (1952), p. 137.

CHAPTER 2

1. US Catholic Conference (1992), p. 98.
2. This argument also applies against McMahan's claim that a "just cause... has to be a goal of a type that can justify killing and maiming." See McMahan (2005b), p. 65.
3. O'Brien (1981), pp. 19–35ff., proceeds in this manner. He also includes, however, right intention in just cause. McMahan (2005b), p. 58, on the other hand, claims that just cause is independent of or prior to proportionality. He says: "I suggest... that just cause says *nothing* about considerations of scale or magnitude but functions entirely as a restriction on the *type* of aim or end that may legitimately be pursued by means of war." In my view, however, he comes nowhere near to providing a plausible argument for that position. He says "that there are numerous worthy and important goals that cannot justify the resort to war, or the practice of war" (ibid.). That is true, but it is true because the war would still be disproportionate. Proportionality is more than importance or worthiness. McMahan would have to provide an example where the war would be disproportionate but nevertheless satisfy just cause. He does not do that. In fact, he even says that, according to the view he accepts, "it might in principle be possible for considerations of proportionality to be fully subsumed within the requirement of just cause" (ibid., p. 57). That, however, is precisely what I say, and it does certainly not suggest an independence or priority of just cause from or to proportionality. So what is his point?
4. Thomson (1991), pp. 293f.
5. Thomson, incidentally, admits this, but goes on to say that a certain argument could be adduced against it. However, since she also admits that she believes this argument to be wrong (and I share her view), it is, on the other hand, "very odd", then, that she does not draw consequences from this, but keeps claiming that the intentions of an actor are irrelevant for the permissibility of the act. See ibid., pp. 294f.
6. Cf. also below, p. 40.
7. Coates (1997), pp. 162f.
8. See O'Brien (1981), pp. 33–5.
9. Cf. Pierce (1996).
10. Paskins and Dockrill (1979), p. 176. Cf. in general, their forceful analyses of the problem of existential dilemmas in war; ibid., pp. 162–8 and 176–81.
11. Cf. also Coates (1997), pp. 179–82.
12. Holmes (1989), Ch. 5, esp. pp. 174ff., and Ch. 6.
13. O'Brien (1981), pp. 28f. Cf. Coates (1997), pp. 176ff.

CHAPTER 3

1. Aquinas (2004), electronic resource.
2. Cf. Davis (1984), p. 108. Walzer (2000), p. 153, demands, as the first condition, that the act be good in itself, "which means, for our purposes, that it is a legitimate act of war". If we know from the beginning that the act is legitimate, why do we need the other conditions? However, many formulations of the principle state the condition that the act be at least not "intrinsically evil". This seems to make more sense, but given the requirement that the agent act with a good intention it is, nevertheless, superfluous. Let us suppose, for example, that murder is intrinsically evil. In that case, the intention of someone who intends to murder a person in order to save many innocent lives is not only to save innocent lives, but to murder. But if murder is intrinsically evil, his intention can hardly be good—it is already compromised. (Note that "good intention" has to be read in an objective sense here. It is not sufficient that S intends to do Y and *believes* that Y is good. Rather, Y has to be, in fact, good.) Be that as it may, whether the condition that the act not be intrinsically evil has to be added to the list of conditions or not is irrelevant for my following criticism of the doctrine of double effect.
3. Anscombe (1970), p. 50.
4. Ibid.
5. Holmes (1989), p. 199.
6. Bennett (1981), p. 100f.
7. Ibid., p. 111.
8. See in particular Mapel (2001), McMahan (1994a), Quinn (1989). Cf. also Davis (1984).
9. Bennett is led down the wrong path on the basis of a supposed analogy between the terror bombing case and another example (Bennett 1981, p. 110). In fact there is no analogy. To discuss this further would, however, be beyond the scope of this book.
10. Nicholson (1978), p. 26, and Coates (1997), p. 244, suggest using (as we shall see, unserviceable) counterfactual test questions (What *would* X say/think if...) to determine what one intends as means. For a criticism, cf. Davis (1984), p. 116f.
11. McMahan (1994a), pp. 202f.
12. Foot (1978), p. 21.
13. Cf. Davis (1984), p. 123, fn. 23.
14. Bennett (1981), p. 109.
15. Davis (1984), p. 115. She applies this problem concretely against what she calls an "agent-interpretation" (ibid., p. 114) of the concept of means.

16. Ibid., p. 115.
17. See Cavanaugh (1999).
18. Cf. Thomson (1991), pp. 290f.
19. Less absolutist proponents of the doctrine of double effect would surely say that B's act is somehow problematic or morally encumbered, but, in light of the proportion of those killed to those saved here, morally allowed. If this is so, then there must be a borderline proportion according to which A's act is allowed, but B's is forbidden. That is, however, just as absurd as the absolutist interpretation.
20. Davis (1984), pp. 118f.
21. Foot (1978), p. 23.
22. See Ch. 4, esp. pp. 82–101.
23. Cf. Locke (2002), p. 287 (*Second Treatise*, § 27).
24. Alexander (1993), p. 58, misconceives this.
25. Cf. Narveson (1970), p. 72.
26. Locke (2002), p. 269–78 (*Second Treatise*, Ch. 2).
27. Cf. Calhoun (2001b), p. 81f.
28. Aquinas (2004), electronic resource (ST II-II, 64.7).
29. Cf. Matthews (1999), p. 68; as well as above, pp. 38f.
30. Aquinas (1953), p. 175.
31. Holmes (1989), p. 181.
32. Ibid., pp. 184–9. Vorobej (1994) tries to refute this premise; the attempt, however, is not very convincing, and it misses Holmes' argument. See on this Holmes (1994).
33. Anscombe (1958), p. 17. For a criticism see Bennett (1966).
34. Holmes (1989), p. 212.
35. Ibid., p. 200.
36. Ibid., p. 201.
37. Ibid., p. 205.
38. Ibid., pp. 201ff., esp. pp. 208f.
39. Belliotti (1995), p. 22, aptly calls it a "legerdemain" and deems it unworthy of further analysis.
40. Holmes (1989), pp. 201–3, points to the moral double standard of certain just war theorists who themselves appeal to the doctrine of double effect but censure its use by pacifists. The comment is justified, but it still does not make similar moral double standards on the pacifist side look any better.
41. Ibid., pp. 203f. His tendency to put the word "cause" in quotation marks at some places hardly veils the fact that one is actually dealing with causes here, and not just with "causes".
42. If Eddie threatens Otto: "If you do not stab yourself to death at once, I will shoot you dead", and Eddie shoots Otto dead following the latter's

refusal to stab himself, then Otto has partially caused his own shooting, but he is hardly morally responsible for being shot.

43. For the considerable problems of this initially so plausible distinction between killing and letting die, see Bennett (1966), pp. 93–7, and (1981), pp. 47–95, as well as Tooley (1980). Malm (1989) shows that the distinction is in *one* respect relevant, after all, but only in one that does not help the pacifist.

44. Belliotti (1995), p. 22.

45. Ibid., p. 23.

46. Holmes (1989), p. 211. Belliotti (1995), p. 25, describes these remarks as "moral sloganism at its worst".

47. Cf. the above discussion of the concept of means on pp. 37ff., in particular the definition on p. 41. I would like to recall that we are only talking of "collateral damages" at the moment, not of direct killings.

48. Holmes (1989), pp. 212f.

49. The idea that rights violations can be justified appears paradoxical to some. See for example Coates (1997), pp. 271f., fn. 39. Nagel (1974), however, shows quite convincingly that there is an indissoluble tension, stemming from moral reality itself, between absolutism (it would be better to speak of a rights-based, deontological morality) and utilitarianism. Similarly Walzer (1974) and (2000), pp. 225–32, 251–63, 323–7. Walzer adheres to the doctrine of double effect, however, and he believes that the rights of innocents are only violated by direct attacks, but justifiably so in extreme cases. On justified rights violations see also the excellent article by Applbaum (1998).

50. Cf. Norman (1995), esp. pp. 197f. and Ch. 6. Norman, to be sure, avoids saying that a war could be justified; instead, he rather talks of "having no choice" and of "necessity". In fact, however, one always has a choice. Instead of killing "in order to prevent some enormous disaster involving huge loss of life" (ibid., p. 208), one can also let the enormous disaster happen. And since one does have a choice, this choice must be justified in order to be morally admissible.

51. Ibid., pp. 197ff.

52. Ibid., pp. 32f.

53. Ibid., pp. 45–7.

CHAPTER 4

1. Anscombe (1970), pp. 44f.
2. Cf. Teichman (1986), p. 65.
3. Murphy (1973), pp. 532–4.

4. Mavrodes (1990), p. 81.
5. Ibid., pp. 82ff. Green (1992) supports a similar approach, extended by Palmer-Fernández (2000). Incidentally, both fail to mention Mavrodes.
6. Norman (1995), pp. 164f.
7. Mavrodes (1990), pp. 82f.
8. Holmes (1989), Ch. 8.
9. Green (1992), p. 57.
10. Norman (1995), p. 165.
11. See Norman (1995), in particular pp. 197f. Also cf. above, Ch. 3, fn. 50.
12. Cf. Walzer (2000), pp. 251ff.
13. This attitude of American politicians and generals as well as of the American public has already been noted by many observers, also, incidentally, by authors who can perhaps be suspected of many things, but certainly not of "Anti-Americanism". David C. Hendrickson (1997), p. 37, for example, an American "realist", that is, an adherent to that school of foreign politics that thinks that a state should, in its foreign politics, rather be guided by its "national interest" than by morality, states: "The central injunction of the war convention is that belligerents have no right to imperil civilian lives. They must not only not aim at the evil effect but also seek to minimize it, accepting risks to their own soldiers. The central injunction of contemporary American strategy, and one which must necessarily be accepted as a condition of public support for an activist American role, is that every measure be taken to minimize the risk of American casualties. It is the latter injunction, not the former, that is going to be controlling in the wars that America fights. That attitude may not be morally appropriate; that it is very powerful seems incontestable." To be sure, there is generally the tendency in Western democracies to want to avoid victims among one's own soldiers, but this tendency is clearly far more pronounced with Americans and leads, in their case, not so much to an abstention from interventions but rather, as I have said, to an abstention from paying much heed to civilians or allied fellow combatants. Cf. Smith (2000), p. 81; *Süddeutsche Zeitung*, 1.4.2003, p. 5 ("Kriegsgericht soll Kritik ahnden. Soldaten erheben Vorwürfe"), and 19.4.2002, S. 8 ("Bin Ladens zaudernde Häscher"). The course of the Iraq war does not give one reason to revise this judgement.
14. Green (1992), p. 41.
15. Ibid., p. 43.
16. Ibid., pp. 51f.
17. Tellingly, there are uncanny parallels with the undemocratic and entirely medieval writings of Francisco de Vitoria, a Dominican writing in the first

half of the sixteenth century, who was of the opinion that "*the entire community can be punished for the sins of its king.* If a king starts an unjust war with another power, the other power to whom injustice has been done can... kill the subjects of the king, even if they are entirely innocent." See Vitoria (1995), p. 139, § 12.

18. Green (1992), p. 51.
19. Locke (2002), p. 388, § 179.
20. Walzer (2000), in particular pp. 34–41 and 296–303. Holmes is of the same opinion. See Holmes (1989), pp. 187f. and (1994), pp. 200f.
21. Cf. McMahan (1994b), p. 214; Nozick (1974), p. 100.
22. Coates (1997), p. 141, fn. 3.
23. Ibid., p. 162.
24. Fullinwider (1990), p. 92.
25. Ibid., pp. 92f.
26. Ibid., p. 94.
27. Alexander (1990), pp. 99f.
28. Ibid., p. 102.
29. Ibid., p. 105.
30. Norman (1995), p. 134. Cf. also Cochran (1996), p. 165.
31. Norman (1995), p. 134.
32. Cf. ibid., pp. 130f.
33. See McMahan (1994b), p. 196; Narveson (1970), p. 74.
34. The correction of distributive injustices can, under certain circumstances, fully justify the use of armed force. In this example, however, distributive injustice is irrelevant—as explicitly stated, Django has no financial duties to this man.
35. Cochran (1996), pp. 163f.
36. Ibid., p. 164.
37. De Roose (1990), p. 166.
38. Thomson (1991), pp. 284 and 287.
39. Thomson (1991), p. 302.
40. Cf. Otsuka (1994), pp. 79ff.; Zohar (1993), p. 608.
41. Zohar's objection (ibid.) that the use of the word "kill" in this context rests on a linguistic ambiguity is inappropriate. The killer firing the bullet at the head of the victim and the bullet perpetrating the victim kill in one and the same sense of "kill"—they bring about the death of the victim. Cf. Thomson (1991), pp. 288f.
42. See above, pp. 45–50.
43. Zohar (1993), pp. 608f.

44. See Otsuka (1994), pp. 93f.
45. De Roose (1990), p. 163. This argument can also be adduced against Rodin (2002), who takes a similar position as Otsuka. Rodin states "that a person's right may be infringed or forfeited only on the basis of something that the person is or does as a moral subject". Ibid., p. 88. In other words, the innocent aggressor or the innocent threat have done nothing to forfeit their right to life, and therefore the potential victim may not defend himself against them. This position, however, is one-sided, for Rodin does not explain what, in turn, the potential victim has done to forfeit his right to defend himself against a threat or an aggressor. And he has this right, as is shown, for example, by the injustice of a law that prohibits destroying a rock that threatens to crush one. In short, not only the innocent aggressor or threat has done nothing to forfeit or diminish their rights, but the potential victim has done nothing of that sort in the relevant examples either. And hence, right stands against right here, which, in the way described above (pp. 85f. and 88f.), leads to the transformation of the relevant rights of the two sides to mere permissions or liberties.
46. See above, p. 55.
47. Otsuka (1994), p. 89.
48. Montague (1989), pp. 81f. The text is a reply to Wasserman's (1987), pp. 365–78, criticism of Montague (1981). Ryan (1983), pp. 515ff. advocates a position similar to Montague's.
49. Hobbes (1994), p. 120. Teichman (1986), pp. 81ff., agrees.
50. According to Wasserman, Paul Robinson takes this position. See Wasserman (1987), pp. 369f.
51. Cf. Montague (1989), p. 87.
52. Bica (1999) overlooks this difference between rights and permissions when he claims that "an act that is permissible never warrants...being the object of the justifiable use of violence and deadly force in self-defence, or in the defense of others." Ibid., p. 132. In fact, this is only true for an act to which one has a *right*, but not for an act which is merely permitted. In addition to our example, this is also shown by the license taken by boxers or duellists to react to an attack with a counter-attack.
53. Cochran (1996), pp. 168f.
54. Cf. Holmes (1989), p. 186.
55. McMahan (1994b), p. 206.
56. Otsuka (1994), p. 91. McMahan, too, has meanwhile adopted this responsibility account of moral liability to defensive killing in place of his earlier

stricter culpability account. See McMahan (2002), esp. pp. 398–421; (2004), esp. p. 696, fn. 10, and pp. 722–72; and (2005), *passim.*

57. Holmes (1989), p. 186.
58. Cf. McMahan (1994b), p. 209.
59. See McMahan (2004), p. 721, and (2005), p. 394.
60. McMahan (2002), p. 405.
61. McMahan (2004), p. 712.
62. McMahan (2005a), p. 399.
63. Ibid., p. 388.
64. Ibid., p. 400.
65. Cochran (1996), p. 169. He refers to Reitan (1994), pp. 119f. and 126f.
66. Ibid., pp. 161f.
67. "Adequate" probably means here "effective and not excessive".
68. See the above discussion of Montague's selection principle, pp. 87f.
69. Fullinwider (1990), pp. 95–7.
70. Cf. Alexy (1985), p. 78.
71. McMahan (1994b), pp. 208f. See also Lauterpacht (1953).
72. See above, p. 61.
73. See above, pp. 59–62.
74. Walzer (2000), p. 187, claims that the distinction between combatants and non-combatants breaks down in every case of mass uprising. Green (1992), p. 53, thinks, however, that Walzer assumes the generality of a distinction that is made questionable by exactly such cases. It seems to me, indeed, that not *every* uprising morally demands the retreat or abdication of the target of the uprising. It depends entirely on the question as to the target of the uprising. If the uprising is against an occupier who spurns the principles of *jus in bello* and who attacks the basic means of living of the population— that is, who fights a war against the populace—then such a withdrawal is the only possible way of avoiding *further* crimes. I say "further", because such attacks on a population's means of living constitute in themselves a crime.
75. Ofer Shelah, *Yediot Aharonot* Saturday Supplement, 19.4.2002, quoted in Reinhart (2002), p. 155.
76. Interview by Tsadok Yehezkeli, *Yediot Aharonot, Seven Days* weekend magazine, 5/31/2002, translated from Hebrew by Gush Shalom; here quoted in Reinhart (2002), pp. 164f.
77. Cf. ibid., p. 155.
78. Ibid., p. 113.
79. Ibid.
80. Ibid., pp. 116–28, 171–80.

CHAPTER 5

1. See Ch. 1.
2. This double standard and abysmal mendacity is documented and criticized with unsurpassable succinctness by the contributions in George (1991).
3. US Department of State (1998), p. vi.
4. Terrorist Research and Analytical Center, National Security Division, Federal Bureau of Investigation, *Terrorism in the United States 1995*, US Department of Justice, Washington, DC, 1996, p. ii; respectively: United States Departments of the Army and the Air Force, *Military Operations in Low Intensity Conflict*, Field Manual 100–20/Air Force Pamphlet 3–20 (Headquarters, Departments of the Army and the Air Force), Washington, DC, 1990; as cited in Hoffman (1998), p. 38.
5. Hoffman (1998), p. 33.
6. Ibid., p. 35.
7. Ibid., pp. 158ff.
8. Coady (1985), p. 52.
9. Held (1991), p. 62.
10. Held (2004), p. 64.
11. Ibid., p. 68.
12. Waldron (2004), pp. 15f.
13. Ibid, p. 14.
14. Ibid., p. 21.
15. Ibid., p. 22.
16. Ibid.
17. Ibid.
18. Ibid., p. 23.
19. Cf. also Rodin (2004), pp. 752–71.
20. O'Neill (2005), p. 15. She adds some other uncertainties to this list, but it is not necessary to enumerate them all here.
21. Ibid., p. 21.
22. Ibid., pp. 21f. Incidentally, if terrorist speech is *by its very nature* elliptical, it is not clear why those who use it must only *for the most part* hide its true nature and import.
23. Schelling (1991), p. 23. Baier (1991), pp. 33–58.
24. Corlett (2003), p. 115, fn. 12.
25. Ibid., p. 115.
26. Ibid., p. 116, fn. 16.
27. Ibid., p. 116.
28. See his definition ibid., pp. 119f.

29. Cf. Primoratz (1990), p. 134.
30. Cf. Walter Sinnott-Armstrong (1991), pp. 115–20.
31. Primoratz (1990), p. 131.
32. Primoratz (1990), p. 129, my emphasis.
33. Rodin (2004), p. 755.
34. Cf. Waldron (2004), p. 9.
35. Against this view Igor Primoratz offers the example "of an insurgent movement that is about to disband or to switch to non-violent politics, but kidnaps some innocent people in order to force the authorities to release their comrades from prison. Wouldn't this be a terrorist act?" (personal communication). The answer is "no", for this case is not different to the one-off hostage-taking I considered above—it simply *is* a case of hostage-taking. One might say that there is a difference between the two cases, because the insurgent movement has political goals. However, Primoratz himself rightly points out that terrorism does not have to be political, it can be criminal. If, then, my example of a one-off hostage-taking that threatens no further acts of hostage taking is not an instance of terrorism—as I think it is not—Primoratz's example is not either.
36. Coady (1985), p. 59.
37. Against this view Igor Primoratz directs the following (rhetorical) question: "Would deliberate killing of civilians by Serb military units in Croatia and Bosnia, performed in secret for the sole purpose of implicating their own soldiers in war crimes and thereby strengthening their loyalty to the cause (a well documented practice), count as terrorism?" (personal communication). I agree that it would not, but this is not a problem for my definition. The means to achieve the aim here is the actual killing of the civilians, not the threat of repeatedly killing civilians.
38. Meggle (2005b), p. 165, translation slightly changed, see the original version, Meggle (2002), p. 153.
39. Meggle (2005b), p. 168. Literally translated "stark zurechenbare Kollateral-Schäden" is "strongly imputable collateral damages", see the German original, Meggle (2002), p. 156.
40. Heller (2002), p. 17, my translation.
41. Here I have corrected a former position of mine in the light of the considerations on pp. 48–50 above. See Steinhoff (2002), p. 193.
42. See above, p. 48.
43. Quoted from Rai (2002), p. 32.
44. Held (1991), pp. 77ff.
45. See above, pp. 57f. and the pertaining fn. 49.
46. Scott (1992), p. 67.
47. Hirschbein (1999), p. 344.

48. Primoratz (1997), p. 231.
49. Ibid., p. 228.
50. See above, pp. 48–50 and pp. 82–150.
51. Held (1991), p. 81.
52. See above, pp. 86f.
53. See above, pp. 62f.
54. See above, pp. 86f.
55. McMahan (1994), pp. 202f.
56. Cf. also the discussion of the criterion of prospects of success above on pp. 29f.
57. Also cf. above, p. 75f.
58. "What We're Fighting For."
59. Walzer (2000), pp. 255–63.
60. Ibid., p. 254.
61. See also Walzer (1990). One must not forget that Walzer is a communitarian.
62. Walzer (2000), p. 254.
63. Valls (2000), p. 73.
64. Walzer (2000), pp. 53–5, 254.
65. See above, pp. 65–7.
66. Baier (1991), p. 54.

References

Lawrence A. Alexander (1990), "Self-Defense and the Killing of Noncombatants: A Reply to Fullinwider", in Beitz et al., pp. 98–105.

—— (1993), "Self-Defense, Justification, and Excuse", *Philosophy & Public Affairs* 22, pp. 53–66.

Robert Alexy (1985), *Theorie der Grundrechte*, Nomos, Baden-Baden.

Gertrude Elizabeth Margaret Anscombe (1958), "Modern Moral Philosophy", *Philosophy* 33, pp. 1–19.

—— (1970), "War and Murder", in: Wasserstrom, pp. 42–53.

Arthur Isak Applbaum (1998), "Are Violations of Rights Ever Right?", *Ethics* 108, pp. 340–66.

Thomas Aquinas (2004), *Summa Theologiae*, http://historymedren.about.com/gi/dynamic/offsite.htm?site=http://www.newadvent.org/summa/,accessedon 5/9/2004.

Annette C. Baier (1991), "Violent demonstrations", in: Frey and Morris, pp. 33–58.

Per Bauhn (2005), "Political Terrorism and the Rules of Just War", in: Meggle, pp. 123–34.

Charles Beitz et al. (eds.) (1990), *International Ethics: A Philosophy & Public Affairs Reader*, Princeton University Press, Princeton.

Raymond A. Belliotti (1995), "Are All Modern Wars Morally Wrong?", *Journal of Social Philosophy* 26(2), pp. 17–31.

Jonathan Bennett (1966), "Whatever the Consequences", *Analysis* 26, pp. 83–102.

—— (1981), "Morality and Consequences", in: Sterling M. McMurrin (ed.), *The Tanner Lectures on Human Values*, Bd. II, University of Utah Press, Salt Lake City, pp. 45–116.

Camillo C. Bica (1999), "Another Perspective on the Doctrine of Double Effect", *Public Affairs Quarterly* 13, pp. 131–9.

Laurie Calhoun (2001a), "The Metaethical Paradox of Just War Theory", *Ethical Theory and Moral Practice* 4, pp. 41–58.

—— (2001b), "Violence and Hypocrisy", *Dissent* 48, pp. 79–85.

Thomas A. Cavanaugh (1999), "Double Effect and the End-Not-Means Principle: A Response to Bennett", *Journal of Applied Philosophy* 16, pp. 181–5.

C. A. J. Coady (1985), "The Morality of Terrorism", *Philosophy* 60, pp. 47–70.

A. J. Coates (1997), *The Ethics of War*, Manchester University Press, Manchester and New York.

David Carroll Cochran (1996), "War-Pacifism", *Social Theory and Practice* 22, pp. 161–80.

Marshall Cohen, Thomas Nagel and Thomas Scanlon (eds.) (1974), *War and Moral Responsibility*, Princeton University Press, Princeton and London.

J. Angelo Corlett (2003), *Terrorism: A Philosophical Analysis*, Kluwer, Dordrecht, Boston and London.

Nancy Davis (1984), "The Doctrine of Double Effect: Problems of Interpretation", *Pacific Philosophical Quarterly* 65, pp. 107–23.

Philippa Foot (1978), "The Problem of Abortion and the Doctrine of the Double Effect", in: id., *Virtues and Vices and Other Essays in Moral Philosophy*, Basil Blackwell, Oxford.

R. G. Frey, Christopher W. Morris (eds.) (1991), *Violence, Terrorism, and Justice*, Cambridge University Press, Cambridge.

Robert K. Fullinwider (1990), "War and Innocence", in: Beitz et al., pp. 90–7.

Alexander George (ed.) (1991), *Western State Terrorism*, Polity Press, Cambridge.

Michael Green (1992), "War, Innocence, and Theories of Sovereignty", *Social Theory and Practice* 18, pp. 39–62.

Virginia Held (1991), "Terrorism, Rights, and Political Goals", in: Frey/Morris, pp. 58–85.

—— (2004), "Terrorism and War", *The Journal of Ethics* 8, pp. 59–75.

Agnes Heller (2002), "Wir kennen unseren Platz in der Welt nicht mehr" (interview with Fritz von Klinggräf), *Freitag*, 22/2/2002, p. 17.

David C. Hendrickson (1997), "In Defense of Realism: A Commentary on Just and Unjust Wars", *Ethics and International Affairs* 11, pp. 19–53.

Ron Hischbein (1999), "A World Without Enemies (Bush's Brush with Morality)", in: Deane C. Curtin, Robert Litke (eds.), *Institutional Violence*, Rodopi, Amsterdam and Atlanta, pp. 343–52.

Thomas Hobbes (1994), *Leviathan, or The Matter, Form, and Power of a Commonwealth Ecclesiastical and Civil* (*The Collected Works of Thomas Hobbes*, Vol. III, ed. by Sir William Molesworth), Routledge, London.

Bruce Hoffman (1998), *Inside Terrorism*, Columbia University Press, New York.

Robert L. Holmes (1989), *On War and Morality*, Princeton University Press, Princeton and Chichester.

—— (1994), "Pacifism and Wartime Innocence: A Response", *Social Theory and Pratice* 20, pp. 193–202.

James Turner Johnson (1984), *Just War Tradition and the Restraint of War: A Moral and Historical Inquiry*, Princeton University Press, Princeton.

Hersch Lauterpacht (1953), "Rules of Warfare in an Unlawful War", in: George Arthur Lipsky (ed.), *Law and Politics in the World Community: Essays on Hans Kelsen's Pure Theory and Related Problems*, University of California Press, Berkeley, pp. 89–113.

John Locke (2002), *Two Treatises of Government*, ed. by Peter Laslett, Cambridge University Press, Cambridge.

H. M. Malm (1989), "Killing, Letting Die, and Simple Conflicts", *Philosophy & Public Affairs* 18, pp. 238–58.

David R. Mapel (2001), "Revising the Doctrine of Double Effect", *Journal of Applied Philosophy* 18, pp. 257–72.

Gareth B. Matthews (1999), "Saint Thomas and the Principle of Double Effect", in: Scott MacDonald, Eleonore Stump (eds.), *Aquinas's Moral Theory: Essays in Honor of Norman Kretzmann*, Cornell University Press, Ithaca and London, pp. 63–78.

George I. Mavrodes (1990), "Conventions and the Morality of War", in: Beitz et al., pp. 75–89.

Jeff McMahan (1994a), "Revising the Doctrine of Double Effect", *Journal of Applied Philosophy* 11, pp. 201–12.

—— (1994b), "Innocence, Self-Defense and Killing in War", *The Journal of Political Philosophy* 2, pp. 193–221.

—— (2002), *The Ethics of Killing: Problems at the Margins of Life*, Oxford University Press, New York.

—— (2004), "The Ethics of Killing in War", *Ethics* 114, pp. 693–733.

—— (2005a), "The Basis Of Moral Liability To Defensive Killing", *Philosophical Issues* 15 (Normativity), pp. 386–405.

—— (2005b), "Just Cause for War", *Ethics & International Affairs* 19(3), pp. 55–75.

Georg Meggle (2002), "Terror & Gegen-Terror. Erste ethische Reflexionen", *Deutsche Zeitschrift für Philosophie* 50, pp. 149–62.

—— (ed.) (2005a), *Ethics of Terrorism & Counter-Terrorism*, Ontos, Frankfurt and Lancaster.

—— (2005b), "Terror & Counter-Terror: Initial Ethical Reflections", in: id., pp. 161–75.

Phillip Montague (1981), "Self-Defense and Choosing among Lives", *Philosophical Studies* 40, pp. 207–19.

—— (1989), "The Morality of Self-Defense: A Reply to Wasserman", *Philosophy & Public Affairs* 18, pp. 81–9.

Jeffrie G. Murphy (1973), "The Killing of the Innocent", *The Monist* 57, pp. 527–50.

Thomas Nagel (1974), "War and Massacre", in: Cohen et al., pp. 3–24.

Jan Narveson (1970), "Pacifism: A Philosophical Analysis", in: Wasserstrom, pp. 63–77.

Susan Teft Nicholson (1978), *Abortion and the Roman Catholic Church*, University of Tennessee Press, Knoxville.

Richard Norman (1995), *Ethics, Killing and War*, Cambridge University Press, Cambridge.

Robert Nozick (1974), *Anarchy, State, and Utopia*, Basic Books, New York.

William V. O'Brien (1981), *The Conduct of Just and Limited War*, Praeger, New York.

Onora O'Neill (2005), "Speech and Terror", unpublished paper.

Michael Otsuka (1994), "Killing the Innocent in Self-Defense", *Philosophy & Public Affairs* 23, pp. 74–94.

Gabriel Palmer-Fernández (2000), "Innocence in War", *International Journal of Applied Philosophy* 14, pp. 161–74.

Barrie Paskins and Michael Dockrill (1979), *The Ethics of War*, University of Minnesota Press, Minneapolis.

Albert C. Pierce (1996), "Just War Principles and Economic Sanctions", *Ethics & International Affairs* 10, pp. 100–13.

Igor Primoratz (1990), "What is Terrorism?", *Journal of Applied Philosophy* 7, pp. 129–38. A revised version of this paper can be found in id. (ed.), *Terrorism: The Philosophical Issues*, Palgrave Macmillan, Basingstoke, pp. 15–27.

—— (1997), "The Morality of Terrorism", *Journal of Applied Philosophy* 14, pp. 221–33.

—— (2001), "What is Terrorism?" This chapter is a newer version of Primoratz (1990).

Warren S. Quinn (1989), "Actions, Intentions, and Consequences: The Doctrine of Double Effect", *Philosophy & Public Affairs* 18, pp. 334–51.

Milan Rai (2002), *War Plan Iraq: Ten Reasons Against War On Iraq*, Verso, London and New York.

Tanya Reinhart (2002), *Israel/Palestine: How to End the War of 1948*, Seven Stories Press, New York.

Eric Reitan (1994), "The Irreconcilability of Pacifism and Just War Theory: A Response to Sterba", *Social Theory and Practice* 20, pp. 117–34.

David Rodin (2002), *War and Self-Defense*, Oxford University Press, Oxford.

—— (2004), "Terrorism without Intention", *Ethics* 114 (July 2004), pp. 752–71.

Frank de Roose (1990), "Self-defence and National Defence", *Journal of Applied Philosophy* 7, pp. 159–68.

Cheyney C. Ryan (1984), "Self-Defence, Pacifism, and the Possibility of Killing", *Ethics* 93, pp. 508–24.

Thomas C. Schelling (1991), "What Purposes Can 'International Terrorism' Serve?", in: Frey and Morris, pp. 18–32.

James C. Scott (1992), "Domination, Acting, and Fantasy", in: Carolyn Nordstrom and JoAnn Martin (eds.), *The Paths to Domination, Resistance, and Terror*, University of California Press, Berkeley, pp. 55–84.

Walter Sinnott-Armstrong (1991), "On Primoratz's Definition of Terrorism", *Journal of Applied Philosophy* 8, pp. 115–20.

Hugh Smith (2000), "The Last Casualty? Public Perceptions of Bearable Cost in a Democracy", in: Michael Evans and Alan Ryan (eds.), *The Human Face of Warfare: Killing, Fear & Chaos in Battle*, Allen & Unwin, St Leonards, pp. 54–83.

Uwe Steinhoff (2002), "Die Ethik des Terrorismus", in: Christian Schicha and Carsten Brosda (eds.), *Medien und Terrorismus. Reaktionen auf den 11. September 2001*, LIT, Münster, pp. 188–97.

Jenny Teichman (1986), *Pacifism and the Just War: A Study in Applied Philosophy*, Basil Blackwell, Oxford and New York.

Janna Thompson (2002), "Terrorism and the Right to Wage War", in: Tony Coady and Michael O'Keefe (eds.), *Terrorism and Justice: Moral Argument in a Threatened World*, Melbourne University Press, Melbourne, pp. 87–96.

—— (2005), "Terrorism, Morality and Right Authority", in: Meggle, pp. 151–60.

Judith Jarvis Thomson (1991), "Self-Defense", *Philosophy & Public Affairs* 20, pp. 283–310.

Michael Tooley (1980), "An Irrelevant Consideration: Killing versus Letting Die", in: Bonnie Steinbock (ed.), *Killing and Letting Die*, Prentice-Hall, Englewood Cliffs, pp. 56–62.

US Catholic Conference (1992), "The Challenge of Peace: God's Promise and Our Response", in: Jean Bethke Elshtain (ed.), *Just War Theory*, New York University Press, New York, pp. 77–168.

US Department of State (1998), *Patterns of Global Terrorism 1997*, Washington, DC.

Andrew Valls (2000), "Can Terrorism Be Justified?", in: id. (ed.), *Ethics in International Affairs: Theories and Cases*, Rowman & Littlefield, Lanham, pp. 65–79.

Franciscus de Victoria (Francisco de Vitoria) (1952), *De Indis Recenter Inventis Et De Jure Belli Hispanorum In Barbaros (Lateinischer Text nebst deutscher Übersetzung)*, ed. by Walter Schätzel), Mohr (Siebeck), Tübingen.

—— (1995), *Vorlesungen I (Relectiones). Völkerrecht, Politik, Kirche*, ed. by Ulrich Horst, Heinz-Gerhard Ustenhoven and Joachim Stüben, Kohlhammer, Stuttgart, Berlin and Köln.

Mark Vorobej (1994), "Pacifism and Wartime Innocence", *Social Theory and Pratice* 20, pp. 171–91.

Jeremy Waldron (2004), "Terrorism and the Uses of Terror", *The Journal of Ethics* 8, pp. 5–35.

Michael Walzer (1974), "Political Action: The Problem of Dirty Hands", in: Cohen et al., pp. 62–82.

Michael Walzer (1990), "The Moral Standing of States", in: Beitz et al., pp. 217–37.

—— (2000), *Just and Unjust Wars: A Moral Argument With Historical Illustrations*, Basic Books, New York.

David Wasserman (1987), "Justifying Self-Defense", *Philosophy & Public Affairs* 16, pp. 356–78.

Richard A. Wasserstrom (ed.) (1970), *War and Morality*, Wadsworth, Belmont.

"What We're Fighting For", www.propositionsonline.com/Fighting_For/ fighting_for/html, accessed on 29/2/2002.

Noam J. Zohar (1993), "Collective War and Individualistic Ethics: Against the Conscription of 'Self-Defense'", *Political Theory* 21, pp. 606–22.

Index

absolutism, moral 52–3, 57, 58, 59, 125
aggressor 34, 45–50, 57, 58, 71, 77, 78–9, 98, 108, 131–2, 134–5
  defined 46
  innocent 80–5, 88–9, 102; *see also* right to attack an aggressor
  non-innocent 86–8, 102; *see also* right to attack an aggressor
Alexander, Lawrence A. 73–5, 89
allowing to die, *see* letting die
anarchy 19–20
Anscombe, Gertrude Elizabeth Margaret 35–6, 52, 61–2, 76, 89, 101
Aquinas, Thomas 19, 34, 38, 51–2
attack 48
Augustine 9

bombing 110
  tactical 37, 96
  terror 37–8, 66
Boyce, Michael 125

causality 54–5
civilian immunity, *see* non-combatant immunity
civilian morale, targeting of 34, 66
Coady, C. F. J. (Tony) 111–21, 122
Coates, A. J. 7–13, 14, 15, 18–20, 27, 69–71, 109
collateral damage 44, 63, 95, 104, 122–3, 125, 131; *see also* doctrine of double effect
combatant 7, 8, 33, 62–101; *see also* non-combatant immunity
convention theory 63–7, 101
consequentialism 56, 128, 129; *see also* rule-utilitarianism; utilitarianism
Corlett, J. Angelo 117–18

danger, present 99–101, 102
democracy 12, 46, 67–71, 123, 131

deterrence 10, 76, 82, 103, 122–5, 135
discrimination, principle of 31; *see also* non-combatant immunity
doctrine of double effect 33–52, 54, 57, 82, 95, 101, 124, 127
double standard(s) 8, 20, 108, 109–10, 133, 137
double targeting 118–19
duty 82, 84, 127

emergency 133–4
  justifying 98–101; *see also* justifying emergency theory; principles, interaction of
  supreme 132–3
excuse 62, 83, 87, 92–3, 94; *see also* responsibility

Foot, Philippa 38–9, 44
Fullinwider, Robert K. 71–6, 89, 101–2

genocide 25, 28, 29, 36, 53–4, 109, 118, 119, 121
Green, Michael 65, 67–8, 76
guilt 8, 54, 57–8; *see also* innocence and non-innocence; moral guilt theory; responsibility

Hiroshima 35, 66, 136
Hobbes, Thomas 87–8
Holmes, Robert L. 52–7, 67, 68, 101
humanitarian intervention 36

innocence and non-innocence 7, 61–108, 121; *see also* guilt; moral guilt theory; non-combatant-immunity
innocents, killing of 23, 24–5, 31, 33–59, 109–37; *see also* innocence and non-innocence; non-combatant immunity
Israel, *see* Palestine

160

Index

jus ad bellum 2–3, 7–31, 62, 94, 108
jus in bello 2–3, 13, 15, 33–108
just cause 12, 13, 14, 16, 23–31
   (esp. 28–31)
justifying emergency theory 101; *see also* emergency, justifying; principles, interaction of

last resort 23, 25, 28–9, 30, 52
laws of war 8, 62, 73, 74, 76, 89, 94, 103, 104, 112
legitimate authority 7–21
letting die 35, 36–7, 53, 55–8, 84
liability 72, 95–7, 103
liberalism 12, 19, 24, 27–8, 30–1, 45, 51, 68–9
Locke, John 19–20, 49, 68

mediated consequences 53–4
Montague, Phillip 87, 107, 130
moral guilt theory 61–3, 101; *see also* principles, interaction of
"moral view", *see* "orthodox view"

Nagasaki, *see* Hiroshima
necessity, *see* emergency
   military 36
non-combatant immunity 7–9, 12, 14, 16, 31–2, 34, 61–108, 134; *see also* innocence and non-innocence
non-innocence, *see* innocence and non-innocence
Norman, Richard 63–7, 76–7
Nozick, Robert 127

O'Neill, Onora 115–17
"orthodox view" 92, 94, 103
Otsuka, Michael 83–4, 85, 94

pacifism 35–7, 48, 52–9, 64, 78–80, 84, 90–1, 98–100
Palestine 8, 12, 15–17, 105–8, 123–4, 131–2, 136–7
principles, interaction of 103–8
proportionality 23, 25, 30–1, 34, 36, 49, 50, 56–9, 95, 96, 100, 101, 125
prospects of success 25, 29–30, 132, 136
punishment 18–19, 49–50, 71, 75–6, 78, 94, 102, 103, 108, 116–17, 122–3, 124, 132

reparation 58
responsibility 53–5, 62, 67–71, 93–7, 107, 123, 130–1, 133, 135
revolution 9–13, 14, 18, 19–20
right(s)
   to attack an aggressor 45–50, 59, 82, 85–8, 90, 93, 101, 128
   to life 46, 50–1, 57, 59, 77, 90–1, 92, 93, 128
   and permissions or liberties 85–6, 88–9
right intention 16, 23, 25–8
Rodin, David 119, 140 n. 34, 147 n. 45
Roose, Frank de 80, 84
rule-utilitarianism 49, 65–7, 101, 103–4, 134

self-defence, *see also* self-defence theory
   individual 34, 38, 49, 71–6
   against innocent aggressors/threats, *see* aggressor, innocent; right to attack an aggressor
   and war 76–99; *see also* principles, interaction of
self-defence theory 101, 71–6; *see also* self-defence; principles, interaction of
self-preservation 83–4
sovereignty 11, 77
success, *see* prospect of success

terrorism
   definition 122
   definitional issues 7–18, 109–22
   assessing 7–18, 122–37
Thompson, Janna 7, 13–18, 109
Thomson, Judith Jarvis 25–6, 81–2, 88
threat, *see* aggressor, innocent

utilitarianism 56–7, 108, 125, 128, 134–5; *see also* consequentialism; rule-utilitarianism

Vietnam 66–7
Vitoria, Francisco de 21, 145 n. 17

Waldron, Jeremy 112–15, 117
Walzer, Michael 67, 68–9, 132–3, 136

5591199